EVERYMAN'S LIBRARY
POCKET POETS

EMERSON

....

POEMS

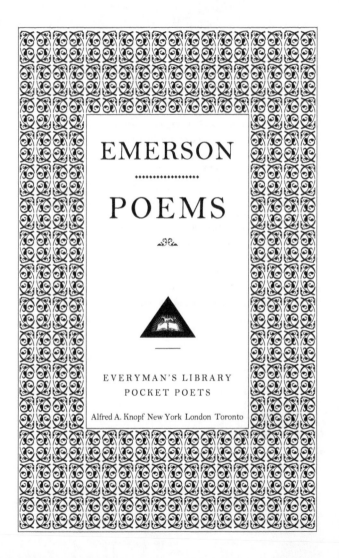

EVERYMAN'S LIBRARY
POCKET POETS

Alfred A. Knopf New York London Toronto

THIS IS A BORZOI BOOK

PUBLISHED BY ALFRED A. KNOPF

This selection by Peter Washington first published in
Everyman's Library, 2004
Copyright © 2004 by Everyman's Library

Eleventh printing (US)

www.randomhouse.com/everymans
www.everymanslibrary.co.uk

ISBN 978-1-4000-4316-3 (US)
978-1-84159-762-1 (UK)

A CIP catalogue record for this book is available from the British Library

Library of Congress Cataloging-in-Publication Data
Emerson, Ralph Waldo, 1803–1882.
[Poems. Selections]
Emerson : poems / edited by Peter Washington.
p.   cm.—(Everyman's library pocket poets)
ISBN 978-1-4000-4316-3 (hc : alk. paper)
I. Washington, Peter.   II. Title.   III. Series.
PS1624.A1   2004   2004046913
811'.3—dc22

Typography by Peter B. Willberg

Typeset in the UK by AccComputing, North Barrow, Somerset

Printed and bound in Germany by GGP Media GmbH, Pössneck

CONTENTS

From *POEMS* (1847)

The Rhodora..	17
The Humble-Bee..	18
Fable	21
Astræa	22
Etienne de la Boéce	24
Suum Cuique..	25
Compensation	25
Forbearance	26
Berrying	26
Thine Eyes Still Shined	27
Eros	27
Loss and Gain	28
Hamatreya	29
The Snow-Storm	32
Painting and Sculpture	33
Holidays	34
From the Persian of Hafiz	35
Ghaselle	41
Xenophanes	43
The Day's Ration	44
Blight..	46
Musketaquid	49
Hymn ('By the rude bridge that arched the flood')	51
The Sphinx	54

Each and All 60
The Problem 62
To Rhea 65
The Visit 68
Uriel 70
The World-Soul 73

From *MAY-DAY AND OTHER PIECES* (1867)

Brahma 81
Nemesis 82
Fate 83
Freedom 84
Ode Sung in the Town Hall 85
Boston Hymn 87
Love and Thought 91
Lover's Petition 92
Una 93
Letters 94
Rubies 95
Merlin's Song 96
The Test 97
Nature I 98
Nature II 99
The Romany Girl 100
My Garden 102
The Titmouse 105
Days 109

Sea-Shore.. 110
Two Rivers 112
Waldeinsamkeit 113
Terminus.. 116
The Past 118
Experience 119
Compensation 120
Culture 121
Politics 122
Heroism 123
Character.. 123
Friendship 124
Beauty 125
Manners 126
Art 127
Spiritual Laws 128
Unity.. 129
Worship 130
Quatrains.. 131

From *SELECTED POEMS* (1876)
The Nun's Aspiration 141
Hymn ('We love the venerable house') 143
Cupido 144
Boston 145
Silence 150
The Three Dimensions 151

Motto to 'The Poet' 151
Motto to 'Gifts' 152
Motto to 'Nature' 152
Motto to 'Nominalist and Realist' 153
Motto to 'History' 153
South Wind 154

From THE UNPUBLISHED POEMS
'William does thy frigid soul' 157
'Perhaps thy lot in life is higher' 158
Song 159
'I spread my gorgeous sail' 160
'O what is Heaven but the fellowship' 161
'Ah strange strange strange' 161
'See yonder leafless trees against the sky' 161
'Do that which you can do' 161
'Few are free' 161
Van Buren 162
The Future 162
Rex 162
'And when I am entombed in my place' 162
'Bard or dunce is blest, but hard' 163
'It takes philosopher or fool' 163
'Tell men what they knew before' 163
'I use the knife' 163
'There is no evil but can speak' 163
'The sea reflects the rosy sky' 163

'In this sour world, O summerwind' 163
'Look danger in the eye it vanishes' 164
'As I walked in the wood' 164
'I sat upon the ground' 165
'Good Charles the spring's adorer' 165
'Around the man who seeks a noble end' 165
'In the deep heart of man a poet dwells' 165
'O what are heroes prophets men' 166
'Yet sometime to the sorrow stricken' 167
The Bohemian Hymn 167
'Kind & holy were the words' 167
'Divine Inviters! I accept' 169
'Go if thou wilt ambrosial Flower' 169
'In Walden wood the chickadee' 170
'Star seer Copernicus' 170
'At last the poet spoke' 170
'I grieve that better souls than mine' 171
Nantasket 171
Water 172
'Where the fungus broad & red' 172
'From the stores of eldest Matter' 175
'And the best gift of God' 175
'Stout Sparta shrined the god of Laughter' 175
'Brother, no decrepitude' 175
'Who knows this or that' 176
'Saadi loved the new & old' 176
'And as the light divided the dark' 176

'When devils bite' 177
'Comfort with a purring cat' 177
'I cannot find a place so lonely' 177
'This shining hour is an edifice' 177
'The sparrow is rich in her nest' 177
'Bended to fops who bent to him' 178
Elizabeth Hoar 178
'Cloud upon cloud' 179
'Since the devil hopping on' 180
'Poets are colorpots' 181
'Thanks to those who go & come' 181
'I must not borrow light' 182
'Comrade of the snow & wind' 182
'God only knew how Saadi dined' 182
'Friends to me are frozen wine' 183
'That each should in his house abide' 183
New England Capitalist 183
'On a raisin stone' 184
'Go out into Nature and plant trees' 184
'Pale Genius roves alone' 185
'Burn your literary verses' 185
'Intellect gravely broods apart on joy' 185
'The civil world will much forgive' 186
'Mask thy wisdom with delight' 186
'Roomy Eternity' 187
Terminus 187
'More sweet than my refrain' 188

'O Boston city lecture-hearing' 188
'A patch of meadow & upland' 188
'And he like me is not too proud' 190
'Park & ponds are good by day' 190
'For Lyra yet shall be the pole' 190
'A score of airy miles will smooth' 190
'All things rehearse' 190
'Pedants all' 191
'I leave the book, I leave the wine' 191
'Easy to match what others do' 191
'If wishes would carry me over the land' 192
Maia 192
'Seyd planted where the deluge ploughed' 192
'Forbore the ant hill, shunned to tread' 192
'Borrow Urania's subtile wings' 193
'The comrade or the book is good' 193
'Is the pace of nature slow?' 193
'Why honor the new men' 193
'Think not the gods receive thy prayer' 194
'Inspired we must forget our books' 194
'Upon a rock yet uncreate' 194

LONGER POEMS
Woodnotes I 197
May-Day 204
The Adirondacs 230

From *The Poet* 244

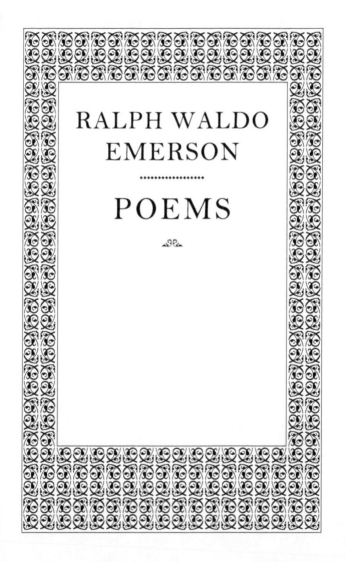

RALPH WALDO EMERSON

POEMS

From
POEMS (1847)

THE RHODORA

On Being Asked, Whence Is the Flower?

In May, when sea-winds pierced our solitudes,
I found the fresh Rhodora in the woods,
Spreading its leafless blooms in a damp nook,
To please the desert and the sluggish brook.
The purple petals, fallen in the pool,
Made the black water with their beauty gay;
Here might the red-bird come his plumes to cool,
And court the flower that cheapens his array.
Rhodora! if the sages ask thee why
This charm is wasted on the earth and sky,
Tell them, dear, that if eyes were made for seeing,
Then Beauty is its own excuse for being:
Why thou wert there, O rival of the rose!
I never thought to ask, I never knew;
But, in my simple ignorance, suppose
The self-same Power that brought me there
        brought you.

THE HUMBLE-BEE

Burly, dozing, humble-bee,
Where thou art is clime for me.
Let them sail for Porto Rique,
Far-off heats through seas to seek;
I will follow thee alone,
Thou animated torrid-zone!
Zigzag steerer, desert cheerer,
Let me chase thy waving lines;
Keep me nearer, me thy hearer,
Singing over shrubs and vines.

Insect lover of the sun,
Joy of thy dominion!
Sailor of the atmosphere;
Swimmer through the waves of air;
Voyager of light and noon;
Epicurean of June;
Wait, I prithee, till I come
Within earshot of thy hum, –
All without is martyrdom.

When the south wind, in May days,
With a net of shining haze
Silvers the horizon wall,
And, with softness touching all,

Tints the human countenance
With a color of romance,
And, infusing subtle heats,
Turns the sod to violets,
Thou, in sunny solitudes,
Rover of the underwoods,
The green silence dost displace
With thy mellow, breezy bass.

Hot midsummer's petted crone,
Sweet to me thy drowsy tone
Tells of countless sunny hours,
Long days, and solid banks of flowers;
Of gulfs of sweetness without bound
In Indian wildernesses found;
Of Syrian peace, immortal leisure,
Firmest cheer, and bird-like pleasure.

Aught unsavory or unclean
Hath my insect never seen;
But violets and bilberry bells,
Maple-sap, and daffodels,
Grass with green flag half-mast high,
Succory to match the sky,
Columbine with horn of honey,

Scented fern, and agrimony,
Clover, catchfly, adder's tongue,
And brier roses, dwelt among;
All beside was unknown waste,
All was picture as he passed.

Wiser far than human seer,
Yellow-breeched philosopher!
Seeing only what is fair,
Sipping only what is sweet,
Thou dost mock at fate and care,
Leave the chaff, and take the wheat.
When the fierce north-western blast
Cools sea and land so far and fast,
Thou already slumberest deep;
Woe and want thou canst outsleep;
Want and woe, which torture us,
Thy sleep makes ridiculous.

FABLE

The mountain and the squirrel
Had a quarrel;
And the former called the latter 'Little Prig.'
Bun replied,
'You are doubtless very big;
But all sorts of things and weather
Must be taken in together,
To make up a year
And a sphere.
And I think it no disgrace
To occupy my place.
If I'm not so large as you,
You are not so small as I,
And not half so spry.
I'll not deny you make
A very pretty squirrel track;
Talents differ; all is well and wisely put;
If I cannot carry forests on my back,
Neither can you crack a nut.'

ASTRÆA

Himself it was who wrote
His rank, and quartered his own coat.
There is no king nor sovereign state
That can fix a hero's rate;
Each to all is venerable,
Cap-a-pie invulnerable,
Until he write, where all eyes rest,
Slave or master on his breast.

I saw men go up and down,
In the country and the town,
With this prayer upon their neck, –
'Judgment and a judge we seek.'
Not to monarchs they repair,
Nor to learned jurist's chair;
But they hurry to their peers,
To their kinsfolk and their dears;
Louder than with speech they pray, –
'What am I? companion, say.'

And the friend not hesitates
To assign just place and mates;
Answers not in word or letter,
Yet is understood the better;
Is to his friend a looking-glass,
Reflects his figure that doth pass.

Every wayfarer he meets
What himself declared repeats,
What himself confessed records,
Sentences him in his words;
The form is his own corporal form,
And his thought the penal worm.

Yet shine forever virgin minds,
Loved by stars and purest winds,
Which, o'er passion throned sedate,
Have not hazarded their state;
Disconcert the searching spy,
Rendering to a curious eye
The durance of a granite ledge
To those who gaze from the sea's edge.
It is there for benefit;
It is there for purging light;
There for purifying storms;
And its depths reflect all forms;
It cannot parley with the mean, –
Pure by impure is not seen.
For there's no sequestered grot,
Lone mountain tarn, or isle forgot,
But Justice, journeying in the sphere,
Daily stoops to harbor there.

ETIENNE DE LA BOÉCE

I serve you not, if you I follow,
Shadowlike, o'er hill and hollow;
And bend my fancy to your leading,
All too nimble for my treading.
When the pilgrimage is done,
And we've the landscape overrun,
I am bitter, vacant, thwarted,
And your heart is unsupported.
Vainly valiant, you have missed
The manhood that should yours resist, –
Its complement; but if I could,
In severe or cordial mood,
Lead you rightly to my altar,
Where the wisest Muses falter,
And worship that world-warming spark
Which dazzles me in midnight dark,
Equalizing small and large,
While the soul it doth surcharge,
That the poor is wealthy grown,
And the hermit never alone, –
The traveller and the road seem one
With the errand to be done, –
That were a man's and lover's part,
That were Freedom's whitest chart.

SUUM CUIQUE

The rain has spoiled the farmer's day;
Shall sorrow put my books away?
   Thereby are two days lost:
Nature shall mind her own affairs;
I will attend my proper cares,
   In rain, or sun, or frost.

COMPENSATION

Why should I keep holiday
   When other men have none?
Why but because, when these are gay,
   I sit and mourn alone?

And why, when mirth unseals all tongues,
   Should mine alone be dumb?
Ah! late I spoke to silent throngs,
   And now their hour is come.

FORBEARANCE

Hast thou named all the birds without a gun?
Loved the wood-rose, and left it on its stalk?
At rich men's tables eaten bread and pulse?
Unarmed, faced danger with a heart of trust?
And loved so well a high behavior,
In man or maid, that thou from speech refrained,
Nobility more nobly to repay?
O, be my friend, and teach me to be thine!

BERRYING

'May be true what I had heard, —
Earth's a howling wilderness,
Truculent with fraud and force,'
Said I, strolling through the pastures,
And along the river-side.
Caught among the blackberry vines,
Feeding on the Ethiops sweet,
Pleasant fancies overtook me.
I said, 'What influence me preferred,
Elect, to dreams thus beautiful?'
The vines replied, 'And didst thou deem
No wisdom to our berries went?'

THINE EYES STILL SHINED

Thine eyes still shined for me, though far
   I lonely roved the land or sea:
As I behold yon evening star,
   Which yet beholds not me.

This morn I climbed the misty hill,
   And roamed the pastures through;
How danced thy form before my path
   Amidst the deep-eyed dew!

When the redbird spread his sable wing,
   And showed his side of flame;
When the rosebud ripened to the rose,
   In both I read thy name.

EROS

The sense of the world is short, —
Long and various the report, —
   To love and be beloved;
Men and gods have not outlearned it;
And, how oft soe'er they've turned it,
   'Tis not to be improved.

LOSS AND GAIN

Virtue runs before the Muse,
  And defies her skill;
She is rapt, and doth refuse
  To wait a painter's will.

Star-adoring, occupied,
  Virtue cannot bend her
Just to please a poet's pride,
  To parade her splendor.

The bard must be with good intent
  No more his, but hers;
Must throw away his pen and paint,
  Kneel with worshippers.

Then, perchance, a sunny ray
  From the heaven of fire,
His lost tools may overpay,
  And better his desire.

HAMATREYA

Minott, Lee, Willard, Hosmer, Meriam, Flint
Possessed the land which rendered to their toil
Hay, corn, roots, hemp, flax, apples, wool, and wood.
Each of these landlords walked amidst his farm,
Saying, "'Tis mine, my children's, and my name's:
How sweet the west wind sounds in my own trees!
How graceful climb those shadows on my hill!
I fancy these pure waters and the flags
Know me, as does my dog: we sympathize;
And, I affirm, my actions smack of the soil.'
Where are these men? Asleep beneath their grounds;
And strangers, fond as they, their furrows plough.
Earth laughs in flowers, to see her boastful boys
Earth-proud, proud of the earth which is not theirs;
Who steer the plough, but cannot steer their feet
Clear of the grave.
They added ridge to valley, brook to pond,
And sighed for all that bounded their domain.
'This suits me for a pasture; that's my park;
We must have clay, lime, gravel, granite-ledge,
And misty lowland, where to go for peat.
The land is well, – lies fairly to the south.
'Tis good, when you have crossed the sea and back,
To find the sitfast acres where you left them.'
Ah! the hot owner sees not Death, who adds
Him to his land, a lump of mould the more.
Hear what the Earth says: –

'Mine and yours;
Mine, not yours.
Earth endures;
Stars abide –
Shine down in the old sea;
Old are the shores;
But where are old men?
I who have seen much,
Such have I never seen.

'The lawyer's deed
Ran sure,
In tail,
To them, and to their heirs
Who shall succeed,
Without fail,
Forevermore.

'Here is the land,
Shaggy with wood,
With its old valley,
Mound, and flood.
But the heritors?
Fled like the flood's foam, –
The lawyer, and the laws,

And the kingdom,
Clean swept herefrom.

'They called me theirs,
Who so controlled me;
Yet every one
Wished to stay, and is gone.
How am I theirs,
If they cannot hold me,
But I hold them?'

When I heard the Earth-song,
I was no longer brave;
My avarice cooled
Like lust in the chill of the grave.

THE SNOW-STORM

   Announced by all the trumpets of the sky,
Arrives the snow, and, driving o'er the fields,
Seems nowhere to alight: the whited air
Hides hills and woods, the river, and the heaven,
And veils the farm-house at the garden's end.
The sled and traveller stopped, the courier's feet
Delayed, all friends shut out, the housemates sit
Around the radiant fireplace, enclosed
In a tumultuous privacy of storm.

   Come see the north wind's masonry.
Out of an unseen quarry evermore
Furnished with tile, the fierce artificer
Curves his white bastions with projected roof
Round every windward stake, or tree, or door.
Speeding, the myriad-handed, his wild work
So fanciful, so savage, nought cares he
For number or proportion. Mockingly,
On coop or kennel he hangs Parian wreaths;
A swan-like form invests the hidden thorn;
Fills up the farmer's lane from wall to wall,
Maugre the farmer's sighs; and, at the gate,
A tapering turret overtops the work.
And when his hours are numbered, and the world
Is all his own, retiring, as he were not,

Leaves, when the sun appears, astonished Art
To mimic in slow structures, stone by stone,
Built in an age, the mad wind's night-work,
The frolic architecture of the snow.

PAINTING AND SCULPTURE

The sinful painter drapes his goddess warm,
   Because she still is naked, being dressed:
The godlike sculptor will not so deform
   Beauty, which limbs and flesh enough invest.

HOLIDAYS

From fall to spring the russet acorn,
  Fruit beloved of maid and boy,
Lent itself beneath the forest,
  To be the children's toy.

Pluck it now! In vain, – thou canst not;
  Its root has pierced yon shady mound;
Toy no longer – it has duties;
  It is anchored in the ground.

Year by year the rose-lipped maiden,
  Playfellow of young and old,
Was frolic sunshine, dear to all men,
  More dear to one than mines of gold.

Whither went the lovely hoyden?
  Disappeared in blessed wife;
Servant to a wooden cradle,
  Living in a baby's life.

Still thou playest; – short vacation
  Fate grants each to stand aside;
Now must thou be man and artist, –
  'Tis the turning of the tide.

FROM THE PERSIAN OF HAFIZ

Butler, fetch the ruby wine
Which with sudden greatness fills us;
Pour for me, who in my spirit
Fail in courage and performance.
Bring this philosophic stone,
Karun's treasure, Noah's age;
Haste, that by thy means I open
All the doors of luck and life.
Bring to me the liquid fire
Zoroaster sought in dust:
To Hafiz, revelling, 'tis allowed
To pray to Matter and to Fire.
Bring the wine of Jamschid's glass,
Which glowed, ere time was, in the Néant;
Bring it me, that through its force
I, as Jamschid, see through worlds.
Wisely said the Kaisar Jamschid,
'The world's not worth a barleycorn:'
Let flute and lyre lordly speak;
Lees of wine outvalue crowns.
Bring me, boy, the veiled beauty,
Who in ill-famed houses sits:
Bring her forth; my honest name
Freely barter I for wine.
Bring me, boy, the fire-water; –

Drinks the lion, the woods burn;
Give it me, that I storm heaven,
And tear the net from the archwolf.
Wine wherewith the Houris teach
Souls the ways of paradise!
On the living coals I'll set it,
And therewith my brain perfume.
Bring me wine, through whose effulgence
Jam and Chosroes yielded light;
Wine, that to the flute I sing
Where is Jam, and where is Kauss.
Bring the blessing of old times, –
Bless the old, departed shahs!
Bring me wine which spendeth lordship,
Wine whose pureness searcheth hearts;
Bring it me, the shah of hearts!
Give me wine to wash me clean
Of the weather-stains of cares,
See the countenance of luck.
Whilst I dwell in spirit-gardens,
Wherefore stand I shackled here?
Lo, this mirror shows me all!
Drunk, I speak of purity,
Beggar, I of lordship speak;
When Hafiz in his revel sings,
Shouteth Sohra in her sphere.

Fear the changes of a day:
Bring wine which increases life.
Since the world is all untrue,
Let the trumpets thee remind
How the crown of Kobad vanished.
Be not certain of the world, –
'Twill not spare to shed thy blood.
Desperate of the world's affair
Came I running to the wine-house.
Bring me wine which maketh glad,
That I may my steed bestride,
Through the course career with Rustem, –
Gallop to my heart's content;
That I reason quite expunge,
And plant banners on the worlds.
Let us make our glasses kiss;
Let us quench the sorrow-cinders.
To-day let us drink together;
Now and *then* will never agree.
Whoso has arranged a banquet
Is with glad mind satisfied,
'Scaping from the snares of Dews.
Woe for youth! 'tis gone in the wind:
Happy he who spent it well!
Bring wine, that I overspring
Both worlds at a single leap.
Stole, at dawn, from glowing spheres

Call of Houris to my sense: –
'O lovely bird, delicious soul,
Spread thy pinions, break thy cage;
Sit on the roof of seven domes,
Where the spirits take their rest.'

In the time of Bisurdschimihr,
Menutscheher's beauty shined.
On the beaker of Nushirvan,
Wrote they once in elder times,
'Hear the counsel; learn from us
Sample of the course of things:
The earth – it is a place of sorrow,
Scanty joys are here below;
Who has nothing has no sorrow.'
Where is Jam, and where his cup?
Solomon and his mirror, where?
Which of the wise masters knows
What time Kauss and Jam existed?
When those heroes left this world,
Left they nothing but their names.
Bind thy heart not to the earth;
When thou goest, come not back;
Fools squander on the world their hearts, –
League with it is feud with heaven:
Never gives it what thou wishest.

A cup of wine imparts the sight
Of the five heaven-domes with nine steps:
Whoso can himself renounce
Without support shall walk thereon; —
Who discreet is is not wise.

Give me, boy, the Kaisar cup,
Which rejoices heart and soul.
Under wine and under cup
Signify we purest love.
Youth like lightning disappears;
Life goes by us as the wind.
Leave the dwelling with six doors,
And the serpent with nine heads;
Life and silver spend thou freely
If thou honorest the soul.
Haste into the other life;
All is vain save God alone.
Give me, boy, this toy of Dæmons:
When the cup of Jam was lost,
Him availed the world no more.
Fetch the wineglass made of ice;
Wake the torpid heart with wine.
Every clod of loam beneath us
Is a skull of Alexander;
Oceans are the blood of princes;
Desert sands the dust of beauties.

More than one Darius was there
Who the whole world overcame;
But, since these gave up the ghost,
Thinkest thou they never were?

Boy, go from me to the shah;
Say to him, 'Shah, crowned as Jam,
Win thou first the poor man's heart,
Then the glass; so know the world.
Empty sorrows from the earth
Canst thou drive away with wine.
Now in thy throne's recent beauty,
In the flowing tide of power,
Moon of fortune, mighty king,
Whose tiara sheddeth lustre,
Peace secure to fish and fowl,
Heart and eye-sparkle to saints; –
Shoreless is the sea of praise;
I content me with a prayer: –
From Nisami's lyric page,
Fairest ornament of speech,
Here a verse will I recite,
Verse more beautiful than pearls:
"More kingdoms wait thy diadem
Than are known to thee by name;
Thee may sovran Destiny
Lead to victory day by day!"'

GHASELLE
from the Persian of Hafiz

Of Paradise, O hermit wise,
  Let us renounce the thought;
Of old therein our names of sin
  Allah recorded not.

Who dear to God on earthly sod
  No corn-grain plants,
The same is glad that life is had,
  Though corn he wants.

O just fakir, with brow austere,
  Forbid me not the vine;
On the first day, poor Hafiz' clay
  Was kneaded up with wine.

Thy mind the mosque and cool kiosk,
  Spare fast and orisons;
Mine me allows the drinking-house,
  And sweet chase of the nuns.

He is no dervise, Heaven slights his service,
  Who shall refuse
There in the banquet to pawn his blanket
  For Schiraz' juice.

Who his friend's skirt or hem of his shirt
    Shall spare to pledge,
To him Eden's bliss and angel's kiss
    Shall want their edge.

Up! Hafiz, grace from high God's face
    Beams on thee pure;
Shy thou not hell, and trust thou well,
    Heaven is secure.

XENOPHANES

By fate, not option, frugal Nature gave
One scent to hyson and to wall-flower,
One sound to pine-groves and to waterfalls,
One aspect to the desert and the lake.
It was her stern necessity: all things
Are of one pattern made; bird, beast, and flower,
Song, picture, form, space, thought, and character,
Deceive us, seeming to be many things,
And are but one. Beheld far off, they differ
As God and devil; bring them to the mind,
They dull its edge with their monotony.
To know one element, explore another,
And in the second reappears the first.
The specious panorama of a year
But multiplies the image of a day, –
A belt of mirrors round a taper's flame;
And universal Nature, through her vast
And crowded whole, an infinite paroquet,
Repeats one note.

THE DAY'S RATION

When I was born,
From all the seas of strength Fate filled a chalice,
Saying, 'This be thy portion, child; this chalice,
Less than a lily's, thou shalt daily draw
From my great arteries, – nor less, nor more.'
All substances the cunning chemist Time
Melts down into that liquor of my life, –
Friends, foes, joys, fortunes, beauty, and disgust.
And whether I am angry or content,
Indebted or insulted, loved or hurt,
All he distils into sidereal wine
And brims my little cup; heedless, alas!
Of all he sheds how little it will hold,
How much runs over on the desert sands.
If a new Muse draw me with splendid ray,
And I uplift myself into its heaven,
The needs of the first sight absorb my blood,
And all the following hours of the day
Drag a ridiculous age.
To-day, when friends approach, and every hour
Brings book, or starbright scroll of genius,
The little cup will hold not a bead more,
And all the costly liquor runs to waste;
Nor gives the jealous lord one diamond drop
So to be husbanded for poorer days.

Why need I volumes, if one word suffice?
Why need I galleries, when a pupil's draught
After the master's sketch fills and o'erfills
My apprehension? why seek Italy,
Who cannot circumnavigate the sea
Of thoughts and things at home, but still adjourn
The nearest matters for a thousand days?

BLIGHT

Give me truths;
For I am weary of the surfaces,
And die of inanition. If I knew
Only the herbs and simples of the wood,
Rue, cinquefoil, gill, vervain, and agrimony,
Blue-vetch, and trillium, hawkweed, sassafras,
Milkweeds, and murky brakes, quaint pipes, and
    sundew,
And rare and virtuous roots, which in these woods
Draw untold juices from the common earth,
Untold, unknown, and I could surely spell
Their fragrance, and their chemistry apply
By sweet affinities to human flesh,
Driving the foe and stablishing the friend, –
O, that were much, and I could be a part
Of the round day, related to the sun
And planted world, and full executor
Of their imperfect functions.
But these young scholars, who invade our hills,
Bold as the engineer who fells the wood,
And travelling often in the cut he makes,
Love not the flower they pluck, and know it not,
And all their botany is Latin names.
The old men studied magic in the flowers,
And human fortunes in astronomy,

And an omnipotence in chemistry,
Preferring things to names, for these were men,
Were unitarians of the united world,
And, wheresoever their clear eye-beams fell,
They caught the footsteps of the SAME. Our eyes
Are armed, but we are strangers to the stars,
And strangers to the mystic beast and bird,
And strangers to the plant and to the mine.
The injured elements say, 'Not in us;'
And night and day, ocean and continent,
Fire, plant, and mineral say, 'Not in us,'
And haughtily return us stare for stare.
For we invade them impiously for gain;
We devastate them unreligiously,
And coldly ask their pottage, not their love.
Therefore they shove us from them, yield to us
Only what to our griping toil is due;
But the sweet affluence of love and song,
The rich results of the divine consents
Of man and earth, of world beloved and lover,
The nectar and ambrosia, are withheld;
And in the midst of spoils and slaves, we thieves
And pirates of the universe, shut out
Daily to a more thin and outward rind,
Turn pale and starve. Therefore, to our sick eyes,

47

The stunted trees look sick, the summer short,
Clouds shade the sun, which will not tan our hay,
And nothing thrives to reach its natural term;
And life, shorn of its venerable length,
Even at its greatest space is a defeat,
And dies in anger that it was a dupe;
And, in its highest noon and wantonness,
Is early frugal, like a beggar's child;
With most unhandsome calculation taught,
Even in the hot pursuit of the best aims
And prizes of ambition, checks its hand,
Like Alpine cataracts frozen as they leaped,
Chilled with a miserly comparison
Of the toy's purchase with the length of life.

MUSKETAQUID

Because I was content with these poor fields,
Low, open meads, slender and sluggish streams,
And found a home in haunts which others scorned,
The partial wood-gods overpaid my love,
And granted me the freedom of their state,
And in their secret senate have prevailed
With the dear, dangerous lords that rule our life,
Made moon and planets parties to their bond,
And through my rock-like, solitary wont
Shot million rays of thought and tenderness.
For me, in showers, in sweeping showers, the spring
Visits the valley; – break away the clouds, –
I bathe in the morn's soft and silvered air,
And loiter willing by yon loitering stream.
Sparrows far off, and nearer, April's bird,
Blue-coated, – flying before from tree to tree,
Courageous, sing a delicate overture
To lead the tardy concert of the year.
Onward and nearer rides the sun of May;
And wide around, the marriage of the plants
Is sweetly solemnized. Then flows amain
The surge of summer's beauty; dell and crag,
Hollow and lake, hill-side, and pine arcade,
Are touched with genius. Yonder ragged cliff
Has thousand faces in a thousand hours.

Beneath low hills, in the broad interval
Through which at will our Indian rivulet
Winds mindful still of sannup and of squaw,
Whose pipe and arrow oft the plough unburies,
Here in pine houses built of new fallen trees,
Supplanters of the tribe, the farmers dwell.
Traveller, to thee, perchance, a tedious road,
Or, it may be, a picture; to these men,
The landscape is an armory of powers,
Which, one by one, they know to draw and use.
They harness beast, bird, insect, to their work;
They prove the virtues of each bed of rock,
And, like the chemist mid his loaded jars,
Draw from each stratum its adapted use
To drug their crops or weapon their arts withal.
They turn the frost upon their chemic heap,
They set the wind to winnow pulse and grain,
They thank the spring-flood for its fertile slime,
And, on cheap summit-levels of the snow,
Slide with the sledge to inaccessible woods
O'er meadows bottomless. So, year by year,
They fight the elements with elements,
(That one would say, meadow and forest walked,
Transmuted in these men to rule their like,)
And by the order in the field disclose
The order regnant in the yeoman's brain.

What these strong masters wrote at large in miles,
I followed in small copy in my acre;
For there's no rood has not a star above it;
The cordial quality of pear or plum
Ascends as gladly in a single tree
As in broad orchards resonant with bees;
And every atom poises for itself,
And for the whole. The gentle deities
Showed me the lore of colors and of sounds,
The innumerable tenements of beauty,
The miracle of generative force,
Far-reaching concords of astronomy
Felt in the plants, and in the punctual birds;
Better, the linked purpose of the whole,
And, chiefest prize, found I true liberty
In the glad home plain-dealing nature gave.
The polite found me impolite; the great
Would mortify me, but in vain; for still
I am a willow of the wilderness,
Loving the wind that bent me. All my hurts
My garden spade can heal. A woodland walk,
A quest of river-grapes, a mocking thrush,
A wild-rose, or rock-loving columbine,
Salve my worst wounds.
For thus the wood-gods murmured in my ear:
'Dost love our manners? Canst thou silent lie?
Canst thou, thy pride forgot, like nature pass

Into the winter night's extinguished mood?
Canst thou shine now, then darkle,
And being latent feel thyself no less?
As, when the all-worshipped moon attracts the eye,
The river, hill, stems, foliage are obscure
Yet envies none, none are unenviable.'

HYMN

Sung at the Completion of the Concord Monument,
April 19, 1836

By the rude bridge that arched the flood,
    Their flag to April's breeze unfurled,
Here once the embattled farmers stood,
    And fired the shot heard round the world.

The foe long since in silence slept;
    Alike the conqueror silent sleeps;
And Time the ruined bridge has swept
    Down the dark stream which seaward creeps.

On this green bank, by this soft stream,
    We set to-day a votive stone;
That memory may their deed redeem,
    When, like our sires, our sons are gone.

Spirit, that made those heroes dare
    To die, or leave their children free,
Bid Time and Nature gently spare
    The shaft we raise to them and thee.

THE SPHINX

The Sphinx is drowsy,
  Her wings are furled;
Her ear is heavy,
  She broods on the world.
'Who'll tell me my secret,
  The ages have kept? –
I awaited the seer,
  While they slumbered and slept; –

'The fate of the man-child;
  The meaning of man;
Known fruit of the unknown;
  Dædalian plan;
Out of sleeping a waking,
  Out of waking a sleep;
Life death overtaking;
  Deep underneath deep?

'Erect as a sunbeam,
  Upspringeth the palm;
The elephant browses,
  Undaunted and calm;
In beautiful motion
  The thrush plies his wings;
Kind leaves of his covert,
  Your silence he sings.

'The waves, unashamed,
   In difference sweet,
Play glad with the breezes,
   Old playfellows meet;
The journeying atoms,
   Primordial wholes,
Firmly draw, firmly drive,
   By their animate poles.

'Sea, earth, air, sound, silence,
   Plant, quadruped, bird,
By one music enchanted,
   One deity stirred, –
Each the other adorning,
   Accompany still;
Night veileth the morning,
   The vapor the hill.

'The babe by its mother
   Lies bathed in joy;
Glide its hours uncounted, –
   The sun is its toy;
Shines the peace of all being,
   Without cloud, in its eyes;
And the sum of the world
   In soft miniature lies.

'But man crouches and blushes,
    Absconds and conceals;
He creepeth and peepeth,
    He palters and steals;
Infirm, melancholy,
    Jealous glancing around,
An oaf, an accomplice,
    He poisons the ground.

'Outspoke the great mother,
    Beholding his fear; –
At the sound of her accents
    Cold shuddered the sphere: –
"Who has drugged my boy's cup?
    Who has mixed my boy's bread?
Who, with sadness and madness,
    Has turned the man-child's head?" '

I heard a poet answer,
    Aloud and cheerfully,
'Say on, sweet Sphinx! thy dirges
    Are pleasant songs to me.
Deep love lieth under
    These pictures of time;
They fade in the light of
    Their meaning sublime.

'The fiend that man harries
  Is love of the Best;
Yawns the pit of the Dragon,
  Lit by rays from the Blest.
The Lethe of nature
  Can't trance him again,
Whose soul sees the perfect,
  Which his eyes seek in vain.

'Profounder, profounder,
  Man's spirit must dive;
To his aye-rolling orbit
  No goal will arrive;
The heavens that now draw him
  With sweetness untold,
Once found, – for new heavens
  He spurneth the old.

'Pride ruined the angels,
  Their shame them restores;
And the joy that is sweetest
  Lurks in stings of remorse.
Have I a lover
  Who is noble and free? –
I would he were nobler
  Than to love me.

'Eterne alternation
    Now follows, now flies;
And under pain, pleasure, –
    Under pleasure, pain lies.
Love works at the centre,
    Heart-heaving alway;
Forth speed the strong pulses
    To the borders of day.

'Dull Sphinx, Jove keep thy five wits!
    Thy sight is growing blear;
Rue, myrrh, and cummin for the Sphinx –
    Her muddy eyes to clear!' –
The old Sphinx bit her thick lip, –
    Said, 'Who taught thee me to name?
I am thy spirit, yoke-fellow,
    Of thine eye I am eyebeam.

'Thou art the unanswered question;
    Couldst see thy proper eye,
Alway it asketh, asketh;
    And each answer is a lie.
So take thy quest through nature,
    It through thousand natures ply;
Ask on, thou clothed eternity;
    Time is the false reply.'

Uprose the merry Sphinx,
    And crouched no more in stone;
She melted into purple cloud,
    She silvered in the moon;
She spired into a yellow flame;
    She flowered in blossoms red;
She flowed into a foaming wave;
    She stood Monadnoc's head.

Thorough a thousand voices
    Spoke the universal dame:
'Who telleth one of my meanings,
    Is master of all I am.'

EACH AND ALL

Little thinks, in the field, yon red-cloaked clown,
Of thee from the hill-top looking down;
The heifer that lows in the upland farm,
Far-heard, lows not thine ear to charm;
The sexton, tolling his bell at noon,
Deems not that great Napoleon
Stops his horse, and lists with delight,
Whilst his files sweep round yon Alpine height;
Nor knowest thou what argument
Thy life to thy neighbor's creed has lent.
All are needed by each one;
Nothing is fair or good alone.
I thought the sparrow's note from heaven,
Singing at dawn on the alder bough;
I brought him home, in his nest, at even;
He sings the song, but it pleases not now,
For I did not bring home the river and sky; –
He sang to my ear, – they sang to my eye.
The delicate shells lay on the shore;
The bubbles of the latest wave
Fresh pearls to their enamel gave;
And the bellowing of the savage sea
Greeted their safe escape to me.
I wiped away the weeds and foam,
I fetched my sea-born treasures home;

But the poor, unsightly, noisome things
Had left their beauty on the shore,
With the sun, and the sand, and the wild uproar.
The lover watched his graceful maid,
As 'mid the virgin train she strayed,
Nor knew her beauty's best attire
Was woven still by the snow-white choir.
At last she came to his hermitage,
Like the bird from the woodlands to the cage; –
The gay enchantment was undone,
A gentle wife, but fairy none.
Then I said, 'I covet truth;
Beauty is unripe childhood's cheat;
I leave it behind with the games of youth.' –
As I spoke, beneath my feet
The ground-pine curled its pretty wreath,
Running over the club-moss burrs;
I inhaled the violet's breath;
Around me stood the oaks and firs;
Pine-cones and acorns lay on the ground,
Over me soared the eternal sky,
Full of light and of deity;
Again I saw, again I heard,
The rolling river, the morning bird; –
Beauty through my senses stole;
I yielded myself to the perfect whole.

THE PROBLEM

I like a church; I like a cowl;
I love a prophet of the soul;
And on my heart monastic aisles
Fall like sweet strains, or pensive smiles;
Yet not for all his faith can see
Would I that cowled churchman be.

Why should the vest on him allure,
Which I could not on me endure?

Not from a vain or shallow thought
His awful Jove young Phidias brought;
Never from lips of cunning fell
The thrilling Delphic oracle;
Out from the heart of nature rolled
The burdens of the Bible old;
The litanies of nations came,
Like the volcano's tongue of flame,
Up from the burning core below, –
The canticles of love and woe;
The hand that rounded Peter's dome,
And groined the aisles of Christian Rome,
Wrought in a sad sincerity;
Himself from God he could not free;
He builded better than he knew; –
The conscious stone to beauty grew.

Know'st thou what wove yon woodbird's nest
Of leaves, and feathers from her breast?
Or how the fish outbuilt her shell,
Painting with morn each annual cell?
Or how the sacred pine-tree adds
To her old leaves new myriads?
Such and so grew these holy piles,
Whilst love and terror laid the tiles.
Earth proudly wears the Parthenon,
As the best gem upon her zone;
And Morning opes with haste her lids,
To gaze upon the Pyramids;
O'er England's abbeys bends the sky,
As on its friends, with kindred eye;
For, out of Thought's interior sphere,
These wonders rose to upper air;
And Nature gladly gave them place,
Adopted them into her race,
And granted them an equal date
With Andes and with Ararat.

These temples grew as grows the grass;
Art might obey, but not surpass.
The passive Master lent his hand
To the vast soul that o'er him planned;

And the same power that reared the shrine,
Bestrode the tribes that knelt within.
Ever the fiery Pentecost
Girds with one flame the countless host,
Trances the heart through chanting choirs,
And through the priest the mind inspires.
The word unto the prophet spoken
Was writ on tables yet unbroken;
The word by seers or sibyls told,
In groves of oak, or fanes of gold,
Still floats upon the morning wind,
Still whispers to the willing mind.
One accent of the Holy Ghost
The heedless world hath never lost.
I know what say the fathers wise, –
The Book itself before me lies,
Old *Chrysostom*, best Augustine,
And he who blent both in his line,
The younger *Golden Lips* or mines,
Taylor, the Shakspeare of divines.
His words are music in my ear,
I see his cowled portrait dear;
And yet, for all his faith could see,
I would not the good bishop be.

TO RHEA

Thee, dear friend, a brother soothes,
Not with flatteries, but truths,
Which tarnish not, but purify
To light which dims the morning's eye.
I have come from the spring-woods,
From the fragrant solitudes; –
Listen what the poplar-tree
And murmuring waters counselled me.

If with love thy heart has burned;
If thy love is unreturned;
Hide thy grief within thy breast,
Though it tear thee unexpressed;
For when love has once departed
From the eyes of the false-hearted,
And one by one has torn off quite
The bandages of purple light;
Though thou wert the loveliest
Form the soul had ever dressed,
Thou shalt seem, in each reply,
A vixen to his altered eye;
Thy softest pleadings seem too bold,
Thy praying lute will seem to scold;
Though thou kept the straightest road,
Yet thou errest far and broad.

But thou shalt do as do the gods
In their cloudless periods;
For of this lore be thou sure, –
Though thou forget, the gods, secure,
Forget never their command,
But make the statute of this land.
As they lead, so follow all,
Ever have done, ever shall.
Warning to the blind and deaf,
'Tis written on the iron leaf,
Who drinks of Cupid's nectar cup
Loveth downward, and not up;
Therefore, who loves, of gods or men,
Shall not by the same be loved again;
His sweetheart's idolatry
Falls, in turn, a new degree.
When a god is once beguiled
By beauty of a mortal child,
And by her radiant youth delighted,
He is not fooled, but warily knoweth
His love shall never be requited.
And thus the wise Immortal doeth. –
'Tis his study and delight
To bless that creature day and night;
From all evils to defend her;
In her lap to pour all splendor;
To ransack earth for riches rare,

And fetch her stars to deck her hair:
He mixes music with her thoughts,
And saddens her with heavenly doubts:
All grace, all good his great heart knows,
Profuse in love, the king bestows:
Saying, 'Hearken! Earth, Sea, Air!
This monument of my despair
Build I to the All-Good, All-Fair.
Not for a private good,
But I, from my beatitude,
Albeit scorned as none was scorned,
Adorn her as was none adorned.
I make this maiden an ensample
To Nature, through her kingdoms ample,
Whereby to model newer races,
Statelier forms, and fairer faces;
To carry man to new degrees
Of power, and of comeliness.
These presents be the hostages
Which I pawn for my release.
See to thyself, O Universe!
Thou art better, and not worse.' —
And the god, having given all,
Is freed forever from his thrall.

THE VISIT

Askest, 'How long thou shalt stay,'
Devastator of the day?
Know, each substance, and relation,
Thorough nature's operation,
Hath its unit, bound, and metre;
And every new compound
Is some product and repeater, –
Product of the early found.
But the unit of the visit,
The encounter of the wise, –
Say, what other metre is it
Than the meeting of the eyes?
Nature poureth into nature
Through the channels of that feature.
Riding on the ray of sight,
More fleet than waves or whirlwinds go,
Or for service, or delight,
Hearts to hearts their meaning show,
Sum their long experience,
And import intelligence.
Single look has drained the breast;
Single moment years confessed.
The duration of a glance
Is the term of convenance,
And, though thy rede be church or state,

Frugal multiples of that.
Speeding Saturn cannot halt;
Linger, – thou shalt rue the fault;
If Love his moment overstay,
Hatred's swift repulsions play.

URIEL

It fell in the ancient periods,
   Which the brooding soul surveys,
Or ever the wild Time coined itself
   Into calendar months and days.

This was the lapse of Uriel,
Which in Paradise befell.
Once, among the Pleiads walking,
Said overheard the young gods talking;
And the treason, too long pent,
To his ears was evident.
The young deities discussed
Laws of form, and metre just,
Orb, quintessence, and sunbeams,
What subsisteth, and what seems.
One, with low tones that decide,
And doubt and reverend use defied,
With a look that solved the sphere,
And stirred the devils everywhere,
Gave his sentiment divine
Against the being of a line.
'Line in nature is not found;
Unit and universe are round;
In vain produced, all rays return;
Evil will bless, and ice will burn.'

As Uriel spoke with piercing eye,
A shudder ran around the sky;
The stern old war-gods shook their heads;
The seraphs frowned from myrtle-beds;
Seemed to the holy festival
The rash word boded ill to all;
The balance-beam of Fate was bent;
The bounds of good and ill were rent;
Strong Hades could not keep his own,
But all slid to confusion.

A sad self-knowledge, withering, fell
On the beauty of Uriel;
In heaven once eminent, the god
Withdrew, that hour, into his cloud;
Whether doomed to long gyration
In the sea of generation,
Or by knowledge grown too bright
To hit the nerve of feebler sight.
Straightway, a forgetting wind
Stole over the celestial kind,
And their lips the secret kept,
If in ashes the fire-seed slept.
But now and then, truth-speaking things
Shamed the angels' veiling wings;

And, shrilling from the solar course,
Or from fruit of chemic force,
Procession of a soul in matter,
Or the speeding change of water,
Or out of the good of evil born,
Came Uriel's voice of cherub scorn,
And a blush tinged the upper sky,
And the gods shook, they knew not why.

THE WORLD-SOUL

Thanks to the morning light,
 Thanks to the foaming sea,
To the uplands of New Hampshire,
 To the green-haired forest free;
Thanks to each man of courage,
 To the maids of holy mind;
To the boy with his games undaunted,
 Who never looks behind.

Cities of proud hotels,
 Houses of rich and great,
Vice nestles in your chambers,
 Beneath your roofs of slate.
It cannot conquer folly,
 Time-and-space-conquering steam;
And the light-outspeeding telegraph
 Bears nothing on its beam.

The politics are base;
 The letters do not cheer;
And 'tis far in the deeps of history,
 The voice that speaketh clear.
Trade and the streets ensnare us,
 Our bodies are weak and worn;
We plot and corrupt each other,
 And we despoil the unborn.

Yet there in the parlor sits
   Some figure of noble guise, –
Our angel, in a stranger's form,
   Or woman's pleading eyes;
Or only a flashing sunbeam
   In at the window-pane;
Or Music pours on mortals
   Its beautiful disdain.

The inevitable morning
   Finds them who in cellars be;
And be sure the all-loving Nature
   Will smile in a factory.
Yon ridge of purple landscape,
   Yon sky between the walls,
Hold all the hidden wonders,
   In scanty intervals.

Alas! the Sprite that haunts us
   Deceives our rash desire;
It whispers of the glorious gods,
   And leaves us in the mire.
We cannot learn the cipher
   That's writ upon our cell;
Stars help us by a mystery
   Which we could never spell.

If but one hero knew it,
    The world would blush in flame;
The sage, till he hit the secret,
    Would hang his head for shame.
But our brothers have not read it,
    Not one has found the key;
And henceforth we are comforted, –
    We are but such as they.

Still, still the secret presses,
    The nearing clouds draw down;
The crimson morning flames into
    The fopperies of the town.
Within, without the idle earth,
    Stars weave eternal rings;
The sun himself shines heartily,
    And shares the joy he brings.

And what if Trade sow cities
    Like shells along the shore,
And thatch with towns the prairie broad,
    With railways ironed o'er? –
They are but sailing foam-bells
    Along Thought's causing stream,
And take their shape and sun-color
    From him that sends the dream.

For Destiny does not like
   To yield to men the helm;
And shoots his thought, by hidden nerves,
   Throughout the solid realm.
The patient Dæmon sits,
   With roses and a shroud;
He has his way, and deals his gifts, –
   But ours is not allowed.

He is no churl nor trifler,
   And his viceroy is none, –
Love-without-weakness, –
   Of Genius sire and son.
And his will is not thwarted;
   The seeds of land and sea
Are the atoms of his body bright,
   And his behest obey.

He serveth the servant,
   The brave he loves amain;
He kills the cripple and the sick,
   And straight begins again.
For gods delight in gods,
   And thrust the weak aside;
To him who scorns their charities,
   Their arms fly open wide.

When the old world is sterile,
    And the ages are effete,
He will from wrecks and sediment
    The fairer world complete.
He forbids to despair;
    His cheeks mantle with mirth;
And the unimagined good of men
    Is yeaning at the birth.

Spring still makes spring in the mind,
    When sixty years are told;
Love wakes anew this throbbing heart,
    And we are never old.
Over the winter glaciers,
    I see the summer glow,
And, through the wild-piled snowdrift,
    The warm rosebuds below.

From
*MAY-DAY AND
OTHER PIECES*
(1867)

BRAHMA

If the red slayer think he slays,
  Or if the slain think he is slain,
They know not well the subtle ways
  I keep, and pass, and turn again.

Far or forgot to me is near;
  Shadow and sunlight are the same;
The vanished gods to me appear;
  And one to me are shame and fame.

They reckon ill who leave me out;
  When me they fly, I am the wings;
I am the doubter and the doubt,
  And I the hymn the Brahmin sings.

The strong gods pine for my abode,
  And pine in vain the sacred Seven;
But thou, meek lover of the good!
  Find me, and turn thy back on heaven.

NEMESIS

Already blushes in thy cheek
The bosom-thought which thou must speak;
The bird, how far it haply roam
By cloud or isle, is flying home;
The maiden fears, and fearing runs
Into the charmed snare she shuns;
And every man, in love or pride,
Of his fate is never wide.

　　Will a woman's fan the ocean smooth?
Or prayers the stony Parcæ sooth,
Or coax the thunder from its mark?
Or tapers light the chaos dark?
In spite of Virtue and the Muse,
Nemesis will have her dues,
And all our struggles and our toils
Tighter wind the giant coils.

FATE

Deep in the man sits fast his fate
To mould his fortunes mean or great:
Unknown to Cromwell as to me
Was Cromwell's measure or degree;
Unknown to him, as to his horse,
If he than his groom be better or worse.
He works, plots, fights, in rude affairs,
With squires, lords, kings, his craft compares,
Till late he learned, through doubt and fear,
Broad England harbored not his peer:
Obeying Time, the last to own
The Genius from its cloudy throne.
For the prevision is allied
Unto the thing so signified;
Or say, the foresight that awaits
Is the same Genius that creates.

FREEDOM

Once I wished I might rehearse
Freedom's pæan in my verse,
That the slave who caught the strain
Should throb until he snapped his chain.
But the Spirit said, 'Not so;
Speak it not, or speak it low;
Name not lightly to be said,
Gift too precious to be prayed,
Passion not to be expressed
But by heaving of the breast:
Yet, – wouldst thou the mountain find
Where this deity is shrined,
Who gives to seas and sunset skies
Their unspent beauty of surprise,
And, when it lists him, waken can
Brute or savage into man;
Or, if in thy heart he shine,
Blends the starry fates with thine,
Draws angels nigh to dwell with thee,
And makes thy thoughts archangels be;
Freedom's secret wilt thou know? –
Counsel not with flesh and blood;
Loiter not for cloak or food;
Right thou feelest, rush to do.'

ODE SUNG IN THE TOWN HALL
Concord, July 4, 1857

O tenderly the haughty day
    Fills his blue urn with fire;
One morn is in the mighty heaven,
    And one in our desire.

The cannon booms from town to town,
    Our pulses are not less,
The joy-bells chime their tidings down,
    Which children's voices bless.

For He that flung the broad blue fold
    O'er-mantling land and sea,
One third part of the sky unrolled
    For the banner of the free.

The men are ripe of Saxon kind
    To build an equal state, –
To take the statute from the mind,
    And make of duty fate.

United States! the ages plead, –
    Present and Past in under-song, –
Go put your creed into your deed,
    Nor speak with double tongue.

For sea and land don't understand,
    Nor skies without a frown
See rights for which the one hand fights
    By the other cloven down.

Be just at home; then write your scroll
    Of honor o'er the sea,
And bid the broad Atlantic roll,
    A ferry of the free.

And, henceforth, there shall be no chain,
    Save underneath the sea
The wires shall murmur through the main
    Sweet songs of LIBERTY.

The conscious stars accord above,
    The waters wild below,
And under, through the cable wove,
    Her fiery errands go.

For He that worketh high and wise,
    Nor pauses in his plan,
Will take the sun out of the skies
    Ere freedom out of man.

BOSTON HYMN
Read in Music Hall, January 1, 1863

The word of the Lord by night
To the watching Pilgrims came,
As they sat by the seaside,
And filled their hearts with flame.

God said, I am tired of kings,
I suffer them no more;
Up to my ear the morning brings
The outrage of the poor.

Think ye I made this ball
A field of havoc and war,
Where tyrants great and tyrants small
Might harry the weak and poor?

My angel, – his name is Freedom, –
Choose him to be your king;
He shall cut pathways east and west,
And fend you with his wing.

Lo! I uncover the land
Which I hid of old time in the West,
As the sculptor uncovers the statue
When he has wrought his best;

I show Columbia, of the rocks
Which dip their foot in the seas,
And soar to the air-borne flocks
Of clouds, and the boreal fleece.

I will divide my goods;
Call in the wretch and slave:
None shall rule but the humble,
And none but Toil shall have.

I will have never a noble,
No lineage counted great;
Fishers and choppers and ploughmen
Shall constitute a state.

Go, cut down trees in the forest,
And trim the straightest boughs;
Cut down trees in the forest,
And build me a wooden house.

Call the people together,
The young men and the sires,
The digger in the harvest field,
Hireling, and him that hires;

And here in a pine state-house
They shall choose men to rule
In every needful faculty,
In church, and state, and school.

Lo, now! if these poor men
Can govern the land and sea,
And make just laws below the sun,
As planets faithful be.

And ye shall succor men;
'Tis nobleness to serve;
Help them who cannot help again:
Beware from right to swerve.

I break your bonds and masterships,
And I unchain the slave:
Free be his heart and hand henceforth
As wind and wandering wave.

I cause from every creature
His proper good to flow:
As much as he is and doeth,
So much he shall bestow.

But, laying hands on another
To coin his labor and sweat,
He goes in pawn to his victim
For eternal years in debt.

To-day unbind the captive,
So only are ye unbound;
Lift up a people from the dust,
Trump of their rescue, sound!

Pay ransom to the owner,
And fill the bag to the brim.
Who is the owner? The slave is owner,
And ever was. Pay him.

O North! give him beauty for rags,
And honor, O South! for his shame;
Nevada! coin thy golden crags
With Freedom's image and name.

Up! and the dusky race
That sat in darkness long, –
Be swift their feet as antelopes,
And as behemoth strong.

Come, East and West and North,
By races, as snow-flakes,
And carry my purpose forth,
Which neither halts nor shakes.

My will fulfilled shall be,
For, in daylight or in dark,
My thunderbolt has eyes to see
His way home to the mark.

LOVE AND THOUGHT

Two well-assorted travellers use
The highway, Eros and the Muse.
From the twins is nothing hidden,
To the pair is naught forbidden;
Hand in hand the comrades go
Every nook of nature through:
Each for other they were born,
Each can other best adorn;
They know one only mortal grief
Past all balsam or relief,
When, by false companions crossed,
The pilgrims have each other lost.

LOVER'S PETITION

Good Heart, that ownest all!
I ask a modest boon and small:
Not of lands and towns the gift, –
Too large a load for me to lift, –
But for one proper creature,
Which geographic eye,
Sweeping the map of Western earth,
Or the Atlantic coast, from Maine
To Powhatan's domain,
Could not descry.
Is 't much to ask in all thy huge creation,
So trivial a part, –
A solitary heart?
Yet count me not of spirit mean,
Or mine a mean demand,
For 't is the concentration
And worth of all the land,
The sister of the sea,
The daughter of the strand,
Composed of air and light,
And of the swart earth-might.
So little to thy poet's prayer
Thy large bounty well can spare.
And yet I think, if she were gone,
The world were better left alone.

UNA

Roving, roving, as it seems,
Una lights my clouded dreams;
Still for journeys she is dressed;
We wander far by east and west.

In the homestead, homely thought;
At my work I ramble not;
If from home chance draw me wide,
Half-seen Una sits beside.

In my house and garden-plot,
Though beloved, I miss her not;
But one I seek in foreign places,
One face explore in foreign faces.

At home a deeper thought may light
The inward sky with chrysolite,
And I greet from far the ray,
Aurora of a dearer day.

But if upon the seas I sail,
Or trundle on the glowing rail,
I am but a thought of hers,
Loveliest of travellers.

So the gentle poet's name
To foreign parts is blown by fame;
Seek him in his native town,
He is hidden and unknown.

LETTERS

Every day brings a ship,
Every ship brings a word;
Well for those who have no fear,
Looking seaward well assured
That the word the vessel brings
Is the word they wish to hear.

RUBIES

They brought me rubies from the mine,
    And held them to the sun;
I said, they are drops of frozen wine
    From Eden's vats that run.

I looked again, – I thought them hearts
    Of friends to friends unknown;
Tides that should warm each neighboring life
    Are locked in sparkling stone.

But fire to thaw that ruddy snow,
    To break enchanted ice,
And give love's scarlet tides to flow, –
    When shall that sun arise?

MERLIN'S SONG

Of Merlin wise I learned a song, –
Sing it low, or sing it loud,
It is mightier than the strong,
And punishes the proud.
I sing it to the surging crowd, –
Good men it will calm and cheer,
Bad men it will chain and cage.
In the heart of the music peals a strain
Which only angels hear;
Whether it waken joy or rage,
Hushed myriads hark in vain,
Yet they who hear it shed their age,
And take their youth again.

THE TEST
(Musa loquitur)

I hung my verses in the wind,
Time and tide their faults may find.
All were winnowed through and through,
Five lines lasted sound and true;
Five were smelted in a pot
Than the South more fierce and hot;
These the siroc could not melt,
Fire their fiercer flaming felt,
And the meaning was more white
Than July's meridian light.
Sunshine cannot bleach the snow,
Nor time unmake what poets know.
Have you eyes to find the five
Which five hundred did survive?

NATURE

I

Winters know
Easily to shed the snow,
And the untaught Spring is wise
In cowslips and anemonies.
Nature, hating art and pains,
Baulks and baffles plotting brains;
Casualty and Surprise
Are the apples of her eyes;
But she dearly loves the poor,
And, by marvel of her own,
Strikes the loud pretender down.
For Nature listens in the rose,
And hearkens in the berry's bell,
To help her friends, to plague her foes,
And like wise God she judges well.
Yet doth much her love excel
To the souls that never fell,
To swains that live in happiness,
And do well because they please,
Who walk in ways that are unfamed,
And feats achieve before they're named.

NATURE

II

She is gamesome and good,
But of mutable mood, –
No dreary repeater now and again,
She will be all things to all men.
She who is old, but nowise feeble,
Pours her power into the people,
Merry and manifold without bar,
Makes and moulds them what they are,
And what they call their city way
Is not their way, but hers,
And what they say they made to-day,
They learned of the oaks and firs.
She spawneth men as mallows fresh,
Hero and maiden, flesh of her flesh;
She drugs her water and her wheat
With the flavors she finds meet,
And gives them what to drink and eat;
And having thus their bread and growth,
They do her bidding, nothing loath.
What's most theirs is not their own,
But borrowed in atoms from iron and stone,
And in their vaunted works of Art
The master-stroke is still her part.

THE ROMANY GIRL

The sun goes down, and with him takes
The coarseness of my poor attire;
The fair moon mounts, and aye the flame
Of Gypsy beauty blazes higher.

Pale Northern girls! you scorn our race;
You captives of your air-tight halls,
Wear out in-doors your sickly days,
But leave us the horizon walls.

And if I take you, dames, to task,
And say it frankly without guile,
Then you are Gypsies in a mask,
And I the lady all the while.

If, on the heath, below the moon,
I court and play with paler blood,
Me false to mine dare whisper none, –
One sallow horseman knows me good.

Go, keep your cheek's rose from the rain,
For teeth and hair with shopmen deal;
My swarthy tint is in the grain,
The rocks and forest know it real.

The wild air bloweth in our lungs,
The keen stars twinkle in our eyes,
The birds gave us our wily tongues,
The panther in our dances flies.

You doubt we read the stars on high,
Nathless we read your fortunes true;
The stars may hide in the upper sky,
But without glass we fathom you.

MY GARDEN

If I could put my woods in song,
And tell what's there enjoyed,
All men would to my gardens throng,
And leave the cities void.

In my plot no tulips blow, –
Snow-loving pines and oaks instead;
And rank the savage maples grow
From spring's faint flush to autumn red.

My garden is a forest ledge
Which older forests bound;
The banks slope down to the blue lake-edge,
Then plunge to depths profound.

Here once the Deluge ploughed,
Laid the terraces, one by one;
Ebbing later whence it flowed,
They bleach and dry in the sun.

The sowers made haste to depart, –
The wind and the birds which sowed it;
Not for fame, nor by rules of art,
Planted these, and tempests flowed it.

Waters that wash my garden side
Play not in Nature's lawful web,
They heed not moon or solar tide, –
Five years elapse from flood to ebb.

Hither hasted, in old time, Jove,
And every god, – none did refuse;
And be sure at last came Love,
And after Love, the Muse.

Keen ears can catch a syllable,
As if one spake to another,
In the hemlocks tall, untamable,
And what the whispering grasses smother.

Æolian harps in the pine
Ring with the song of the Fates;
Infant Bacchus in the vine, –
Far distant yet his chorus waits.

Canst thou copy in verse one chime
Of the wood-bell's peal and cry,
Write in a book the morning's prime,
Or match with words that tender sky?

Wonderful verse of the gods,
Of one import, of varied tone;
They chant the bliss of their abodes
To man imprisoned in his own.

Ever the words of the gods resound;
But the porches of man's ear
Seldom in this low life's round
Are unsealed, that he may hear.

Wandering voices in the air,
And murmurs in the wold,
Speak what I cannot declare,
Yet cannot all withhold.

When the shadow fell on the lake,
The whirlwind in ripples wrote
Air-bells of fortune that shine and break,
And omens above thought.

But the meanings cleave to the lake,
Cannot be carried in book or urn;
Go thy ways now, come later back,
On waves and hedges still they burn.

These the fates of men forecast,
Of better men than live to-day;
If who can read them comes at last,
He will spell in the sculpture, 'Stay!'

THE TITMOUSE

You shall not be overbold
When you deal with arctic cold,
As late I found my lukewarm blood
Chilled wading in the snow-choked wood.
How should I fight? my foeman fine
Has million arms to one of mine:
East, west, for aid I looked in vain,
East, west, north, south, are his domain.
Miles off, three dangerous miles, is home;
Must borrow his winds who there would come.
Up and away for life! be fleet! –
The frost-king ties my fumbling feet,
Sings in my ears, my hands are stones,
Curdles the blood to the marble bones,
Tugs at the heart-strings, numbs the sense,
And hems in life with narrowing fence.
Well, in this broad bed lie and sleep,
The punctual stars will vigil keep,
Embalmed by purifying cold,
The winds shall sing their dead-march old,
The snow is no ignoble shroud,
The moon thy mourner, and the cloud.

Softly, – but this way fate was pointing,
'T was coming fast to such anointing,

When piped a tiny voice hard by,
Gay and polite, a cheerful cry,
Chic-chicadeedee! saucy note
Out of sound heart and merry throat,
As if it said, 'Good day, good sir!
Fine afternoon, old passenger!
Happy to meet you in these places,
Where January brings few faces.'

This poet, though he live apart,
Moved by his hospitable heart,
Sped, when I passed his sylvan fort,
To do the honors of his court,
As fits a feathered lord of land;
Flew near, with soft wing grazed my hand,
Hopped on the bough, then, darting low,
Prints his small impress on the snow,
Shows feats of his gymnastic play,
Head downward, clinging to the spray.

Here was this atom in full breath,
Hurling defiance at vast death;
This scrap of valor just for play
Fronts the north-wind in waistcoat gray,
As if to shame my weak behavior;
I greeted loud my little saviour,
'You pet! what dost here? and what for?

In these woods, thy small Labrador,
At this pinch, wee San Salvador!
What fire burns in that little chest
So frolic, stout, and self-possest?
Henceforth I wear no stripe but thine;
Ashes and jet all hues outshine.
Why are not diamonds black and gray,
To ape thy dare-devil array?
And I affirm, the spacious North
Exists to draw thy virtue forth.
I think no virtue goes with size;
The reason of all cowardice
Is, that men are overgrown,
And, to be valiant, must come down
To the titmouse dimension.'

'Tis good-will makes intelligence,
And I began to catch the sense
Of my bird's song: 'Live out of doors
In the great woods, on prairie floors.
I dine in the sun; when he sinks in the sea,
I too have a hole in a hollow tree;
And I like less when Summer beats
With stifling beams on these retreats,
Than noontide twilights which snow makes
With tempest of the blinding flakes.
For well the soul, if stout within,

Can arm impregnably the skin;
And polar frost my frame defied,
Made of the air that blows outside.'

With glad remembrance of my debt,
I homeward turn; farewell, my pet!
When here again thy pilgrim comes,
He shall bring store of seeds and crumbs.
Doubt not, so long as earth has bread,
Thou first and foremost shalt be fed;
The Providence that is most large
Takes hearts like thine in special charge,
Helps who for their own need are strong,
And the sky doats on cheerful song.
Henceforth I prize thy wiry chant
O'er all that mass and minster vaunt;
For men mis-hear thy call in spring,
As 't would accost some frivolous wing,
Crying out of the hazel copse, *Phe-be!*
And, in winter, *Chic-a-dee-dee!*
I think old Cæsar must have heard
In northern Gaul my dauntless bird,
And, echoed in some frosty wold,
Borrowed thy battle-numbers bold.
And I will write our annals new,
And thank thee for a better clew,
I, who dreamed not when I came here

To find the antidote of fear,
Now hear thee say in Roman key,
Pæan! Veni, vidi, vici.

DAYS

Daughters of Time, the hypocritic Days,
Muffled and dumb like barefoot dervishes,
And marching single in an endless file,
Bring diadems and fagots in their hands.
To each they offer gifts after his will,
Bread, kingdoms, stars, and sky that holds them all.
I, in my pleached garden, watched the pomp,
Forgot my morning wishes, hastily
Took a few herbs and apples, and the Day
Turned and departed silent. I, too late,
Under her solemn fillet saw the scorn.

SEA-SHORE

I heard or seemed to hear the chiding Sea
Say, Pilgrim, why so late and slow to come?
Am I not always here, thy summer home?
Is not my voice thy music, morn and eve?
My breath thy healthful climate in the heats,
My touch thy antidote, my bay thy bath?
Was ever building like my terraces?
Was ever couch magnificent as mine?
Lie on the warm rock-ledges, and there learn
A little hut suffices like a town.
I make your sculptured architecture vain,
Vain beside mine. I drive my wedges home,
And carve the coastwise mountain into caves.
Lo! here is Rome, and Nineveh, and Thebes,
Karnak, and Pyramid, and Giant's Stairs,
Half piled or prostrate; and my newest slab
Older than all thy race.

                            Behold the Sea,
The opaline, the plentiful and strong,
Yet beautiful as is the rose in June,
Fresh as the trickling rainbow of July;
Sea full of food, the nourisher of kinds,
Purger of earth, and medicine of men;
Creating a sweet climate by my breath,
Washing out harms and griefs from memory,

And, in my mathematic ebb and flow,
Giving a hint of that which changes not.
Rich are the sea-gods: – who gives gifts but they?
They grope the sea for pearls, but more than pearls:
They pluck Force thence, and give it to the wise.
For every wave is wealth to Dædalus,
Wealth to the cunning artist who can work
This matchless strength. Where shall he find, O waves!
A load your Atlas shoulders cannot lift?

   I with my hammer pounding evermore
The rocky coast, smite Andes into dust,
Strewing my bed, and, in another age,
Rebuild a continent of better men.
Then I unbar the doors: my paths lead out
The exodus of nations: I disperse
Men to all shores that front the hoary main.

   I too have arts and sorceries;
Illusion dwells forever with the wave.
I know what spells are laid. Leave me to deal
With credulous and imaginative man;
For, though he scoop my water in his palm,
A few rods off he deems it gems and clouds.
Planting strange fruits and sunshine on the shore,
I make some coast alluring, some lone isle,
To distant men, who must go there, or die.

TWO RIVERS

Thy summer voice, Musketaquit,
Repeats the music of the rain;
But sweeter rivers pulsing flit
Through thee, as thou through Concord Plain.

Thou in thy narrow banks art pent:
The stream I love unbounded goes
Through flood and sea and firmament;
Through light, through life, it forward flows.

I see the inundation sweet,
I hear the spending of the stream
Through years, through men, through nature fleet,
Through passion, thought, through power and dream.

Musketaquit, a goblin strong,
Of shard and flint makes jewels gay;
They lose their grief who hear his song,
And where he winds is the day of day.

So forth and brighter fares my stream, –
Who drink it shall not thirst again;
No darkness stains its equal gleam,
And ages drop in it like rain.

WALDEINSAMKEIT

I do not count the hours I spend
In wandering by the sea;
The forest is my loyal friend,
Like God it useth me.

In plains that room for shadows make
Of skirting hills to lie,
Bound in by streams which give and take
Their colors from the sky;

Or on the mountain-crest sublime,
Or down the oaken glade,
O what have I to do with time?
For this the day was made.

Cities of mortals woe-begone
Fantastic care derides,
But in the serious landscape lone
Stern benefit abides.

Sheen will tarnish, honey cloy,
And merry is only a mask of sad,
But, sober on a fund of joy,
The woods at heart are glad.

There the great Planter plants
Of fruitful worlds the grain,
And with a million spells enchants
The souls that walk in pain.

Still on the seeds of all he made
The rose of beauty burns;
Through times that wear, and forms that fade,
Immortal youth returns.

The black ducks mounting from the lake,
The pigeon in the pines,
The bittern's boom, a desert make
Which no false art refines.

Down in yon watery nook,
Where bearded mists divide,
The gray old gods whom Chaos knew,
The sires of Nature, hide.

Aloft, in secret veins of air,
Blows the sweet breath of song,
O, few to scale those uplands dare,
Though they to all belong!

See thou bring not to field or stone
The fancies found in books;
Leave authors' eyes, and fetch your own,
To brave the landscape's looks.

And if, amid this dear delight,
My thoughts did home rebound,
I well might reckon it a slight
To the high cheer I found.

Oblivion here thy wisdom is,
Thy thrift, the sleep of cares;
For a proud idleness like this
Crowns all thy mean affairs.

TERMINUS

It is time to be old,
To take in sail: –
The god of bounds,
Who sets to seas a shore,
Came to me in his fatal rounds,
And said: 'No more!
No farther spread
Thy broad ambitious branches, and thy root.
Fancy departs: no more invent,
Contract thy firmament
To compass of a tent.
There's not enough for this and that,
Make thy option which of two;
Economize the falling river,
Not the less revere the Giver,
Leave the many and hold the few.
Timely wise accept the terms,
Soften the fall with wary foot;
A little while
Still plan and smile,
And, fault of novel germs,
Mature the unfallen fruit.
Curse, if thou wilt, thy sires,
Bad husbands of their fires,
Who, when they gave thee breath,

Failed to bequeath
The needful sinew stark as once,
The Baresark marrow to thy bones,
But left a legacy of ebbing veins,
Inconstant heat and nerveless reins, –
Amid the Muses, left thee deaf and dumb,
Amid the gladiators, halt and numb.'

As the bird trims her to the gale,
I trim myself to the storm of time,
I man the rudder, reef the sail,
Obey the voice at eve obeyed at prime:
'Lowly faithful, banish fear,
Right onward drive unharmed;
The port, well worth the cruise, is near,
And every wave is charmed.'

THE PAST

The debt is paid,
The verdict said,
The Furies laid,
The plague is stayed,
All fortunes made;
Turn the key and bolt the door,
Sweet is death forevermore.
Nor haughty hope, nor swart chagrin,
Nor murdering hate, can enter in.
All is now secure and fast;
Not the gods can shake the Past;
Flies-to the adamantine door
Bolted down forevermore.
None can re-enter there, –
No thief so politic,
No Satan with a royal trick
Steal in by window, chink, or hole,
To bind or unbind, add what lacked,
Insert a leaf, or forge a name,
New-face or finish what is packed,
Alter or mend eternal Fact.

EXPERIENCE

The lords of life, the lords of life, –
I saw them pass,
In their own guise,
Like and unlike,
Portly and grim, –
Use and Surprise,
Surface and Dream,
Succession swift and spectral Wrong,
Temperament without a tongue,
And the inventor of the game
Omnipresent without name; –
Some to see, some to be guessed,
They marched from east to west:
Little man, least of all,
Among the legs of his guardians tall,
Walked about with puzzled look.
Him by the hand dear Nature took,
Dearest Nature, strong and kind,
Whispered, 'Darling, never mind!
To-morrow they will wear another face,
The founder thou; these are thy race!'

COMPENSATION

I

The wings of Time are black and white,
Pied with morning and with night.
Mountain tall and ocean deep
Trembling balance duly keep.
In changing moon and tidal wave
Glows the feud of Want and Have.
Gauge of more and less through space,
Electric star or pencil plays,
The lonely Earth amid the balls
That hurry through the eternal halls,
A makeweight flying to the void,
Supplemental asteroid,
Or compensatory spark,
Shoots across the neutral Dark.

II

Man's the elm, and Wealth the vine;
Stanch and strong the tendrils twine:
Though the frail ringlets thee deceive,
None from its stock that vine can reave.
Fear not, then, thou child infirm,
There's no god dare wrong a worm;
Laurel crowns cleave to deserts,
And power to him who power exerts.

Hast not thy share? On winged feet,
Lo! it rushes thee to meet;
And all that Nature made thy own,
Floating in air or pent in stone,
Will rive the hills and swim the sea,
And, like thy shadow, follow thee.

CULTURE

Can rules or tutors educate
The semigod whom we await?
He must be musical,
Tremulous, impressional,
Alive to gentle influence
Of landscape and of sky,
And tender to the spirit-touch
Of man's or maiden's eye:
But, to his native centre fast,
Shall into Future fuse the Past,
And the world's flowing fates in his own mould recast.

POLITICS

Gold and iron are good
To buy iron and gold;
All earth's fleece and food
For their like are sold.
Hinted Merlin wise,
Proved Napoleon great,
Nor kind nor coinage buys
Aught above its rate.
Fear, Craft, and Avarice
Cannot rear a State.
Out of dust to build
What is more than dust, –
Walls Amphion piled
Phœbus stablish must.
When the Muses nine
With the Virtues meet,
Find to their design
An Atlantic seat,
By green orchard boughs
Fended from the heat,
Where the statesman ploughs
Furrow for the wheat, –
When the Church is social worth,
When the state-house is the hearth,
Then the perfect State is come,
The republican at home.

HEROISM

Ruby wine is drunk by knaves,
Sugar spends to fatten slaves,
Rose and vine-leaf deck buffoons;
Thunder-clouds are Jove's festoons,
Drooping oft in wreaths of dread,
Lightning-knotted round his head;
The hero is not fed on sweets,
Daily his own heart he eats;
Chambers of the great are jails,
And head-winds right for royal sails.

CHARACTER

The sun set, but set not his hope:
Stars rose; his faith was earlier up:
Fixed on the enormous galaxy,
Deeper and older seemed his eye;
And matched his sufferance sublime
The taciturnity of time.
He spoke, and words more soft than rain
Brought the Age of Gold again:
His action won such reverence sweet
As hid all measure of the feat.

FRIENDSHIP

A ruddy drop of manly blood
The surging sea outweighs,
The world uncertain comes and goes,
The lover rooted stays.
I fancied he was fled, —
And, after many a year,
Glowed unexhausted kindliness,
Like daily sunrise there.
My careful heart was free again,
O friend, my bosom said,
Through thee alone the sky is arched,
Through thee the rose is red;
All things through thee take nobler form,
And look beyond the earth,
The mill-round of our fate appears
A sun-path in thy worth.
Me too thy nobleness has taught
To master my despair;
The fountains of my hidden life
Are through thy friendship fair.

BEAUTY

Was never form and never face
So sweet to SEYD as only grace
Which did not slumber like a stone,
But hovered gleaming and was gone.
Beauty chased he everywhere,
In flame, in storm, in clouds of air.
He smote the lake to feed his eye
With the beryl beam of the broken wave;
He flung in pebbles well to hear
The moment's music which they gave.
Oft pealed for him a lofty tone
From nodding pole and belting zone.
He heard a voice none else could hear
From centred and from errant sphere.
The quaking earth did quake in rhyme,
Seas ebbed and flowed in epic chime.
In dens of passion, and pits of woe,
He saw strong Eros struggling through,
To sun the dark and solve the curse,
And beam to the bounds of the universe.
While thus to love he gave his days
In loyal worship, scorning praise,
How spread their lures for him in vain
Thieving Ambition and paltering Gain!
He thought it happier to be dead,
To die for Beauty, than live for bread.

MANNERS

Grace, Beauty, and Caprice
Build this golden portal;
Graceful women, chosen men,
Dazzle every mortal.
Their sweet and lofty countenance
His enchanted food;
He need not go to them, their forms
Beset his solitude.
He looketh seldom in their face,
His eyes explore the ground, –
The green grass is a looking-glass
Whereon their traits are found.
Little and less he says to them,
So dances his heart in his breast;
Their tranquil mien bereaveth him
Of wit, of words, of rest.
Too weak to win, too fond to shun
The tyrants of his doom,
The much deceived Endymion
Slips behind a tomb.

ART

Give to barrows, trays, and pans
Grace and glimmer of romance;
Bring the moonlight into noon
Hid in gleaming piles of stone;
On the city's paved street
Plant gardens lined with lilacs sweet;
Let spouting fountains cool the air,
Singing in the sun-baked square;
Let statue, picture, park, and hall,
Ballad, flag, and festival,
The past restore, the day adorn,
And make to-morrow a new morn.
So shall the drudge in dusty frock
Spy behind the city clock
Retinues of airy kings,
Skirts of angels, starry wings,
His fathers shining in bright fables,
His children fed at heavenly tables.
'Tis the privilege of Art
Thus to play its cheerful part,
Man on earth to acclimate,
And bend the exile to his fate,
And, moulded of one element
With the days and firmament,
Teach him on these as stairs to climb,

And live on even terms with Time;
Whilst upper life the slender rill
Of human sense doth overfill.

SPIRITUAL LAWS

The living Heaven thy prayers respect,
House at once and architect,
Quarrying man's rejected hours,
Builds therewith eternal towers;
Sole and self-commanded works,
Fears not undermining days,
Grows by decays,
And, by the famous might that lurks
In reaction and recoil,
Makes flame to freeze, and ice to boil;
Forging, through swart arms of Offence,
The silver seat of Innocence.

UNITY

Space is ample, east and west,
But two cannot go abreast,
Cannot travel in it two:
Yonder masterful cuckoo
Crowds every egg out of the nest,
Quick or dead, except its own;
A spell is laid on sod and stone,
Night and Day were tampered with,
Every quality and pith
Surcharged and sultry with a power
That works its will on age and hour.

WORSHIP

This is he, who, felled by foes,
Sprung harmless up, refreshed by blows:
He to captivity was sold,
But him no prison-bars would hold:
Though they sealed him in a rock,
Mountain chains he can unlock:
Thrown to lions for their meat,
The crouching lion kissed his feet:
Bound to the stake, no flames appalled,
But arched o'er him an honoring vault.
This is he men miscall Fate,
Threading dark ways, arriving late,
But ever coming in time to crown
The truth, and hurl wrong-doers down.
He is the oldest, and best known,
More near than aught thou call'st thy own,
Yet, greeted in another's eyes,
Disconcerts with glad surprise.
This is Jove, who, deaf to prayers,
Floods with blessings unawares.
Draw, if thou canst, the mystic line
Severing rightly his from thine,
Which is human, which divine.

QUATRAINS

S.H.

With beams December planets dart
His cold eye truth and conduct scanned,
July was in his sunny heart,
October in his liberal hand.

A.H.

High was her heart, and yet was well inclined,
Her manners made of bounty well refined;
Far capitals, and marble courts, her eye still seemed
    to see,
Minstrels, and kings, and high-born dames, and of
    the best that be.

'Suum Cuique'

Wilt thou seal up the avenues of ill?
Pay every debt, as if God wrote the bill.

Hush!

Every thought is public,
Every nook is wide;
Thy gossips spread each whisper,
And the gods from side to side.

Orator

He who has no hands
Perforce must use his tongue;
Foxes are so cunning
Because they are not strong.

Artist

Quit the hut, frequent the palace,
Reck not what the people say;
For still, where'er the trees grow biggest,
Huntsmen find the easiest way.

Poet

Ever the Poet *from* the land
Steers his bark, and trims his sail;
Right out to sea his courses stand,
New worlds to find in pinnace frail.

Poet

To clothe the fiery thought
In simple words succeeds,
For still the craft of genius is
To mask a king in weeds.

Botanist

Go thou to thy learned task,
I stay with the flowers of spring:
Do thou of the ages ask
What me the hours will bring.

Gardener

True Bramin, in the morning meadows wet,
Expound the Vedas of the violet,
Or, hid in vines, peeping through many a loop,
See the plum redden, and the beurré stoop.

Forester

He took the color of his vest
From rabbit's coat or grouse's breast;
For, as the wood-kinds lurk and hide,
So walks the woodman, unespied.

Northman

The gale that wrecked you on the sand,
It helped my rowers to row;
The storm is my best galley hand,
And drives me where I go.

From Alcuin

The sea is the road of the bold,
Frontier of the wheat-sown plains,
The pit wherein the streams are rolled,
And fountain of the rains.

Excelsior

Over his head were the maple buds,
And over the tree was the moon,
And over the moon were the starry studs,
That drop from the angels' shoon.

Borrowing
From the French

Some of your hurts you have cured,
And the sharpest you still have survived,
But what torments of grief you endured
From evils which never arrived!

Nature

Boon Nature yields each day a brag which we now
    first behold,
And trains us on to slight the new, as if it were the old:
But blest is he, who, playing deep, yet haply asks not
    why,
Too busied with the crowded hour to fear to live or die.

Fate

Her planted eye to-day controls,
Is in the morrow most at home,
And sternly calls to being souls
That curse her when they come.

Horoscope

Ere he was born, the stars of fate
Plotted to make him rich and great:
When from the womb the babe was loosed,
The gate of gifts behind him closed.

Power

Cast the bantling on the rocks,
Suckle him with the she-wolf's teat,
Wintered with the hawk and fox,
Power and speed be hands and feet.

Climacteric

I am not wiser for my age,
Nor skilful by my grief;
Life loiters at the book's first page, –
Ah! could we turn the leaf.

Heri, Cras, Hodie

Shines the last age, the next with hope is seen,
To-day slinks poorly off unmarked between:
Future or Past no richer secret folds,
O friendless Present! than thy bosom holds.

Memory

Night-dreams trace on Memory's wall
Shadows of the thoughts of day,
And thy fortunes, as they fall,
The bias of the will betray.

Love

Love on his errand bound to go
Can swim the flood, and wade through snow,
Where way is none, 't will creep and wind
And eat through Alps its home to find.

Sacrifice

Though love repine, and reason chafe,
There came a voice without reply, –
'"Tis man's perdition to be safe,
When for the truth he ought to die.'

Pericles

Well and wisely said the Greek,
Be thou faithful, but not fond;
To the altar's foot thy fellow seek,
The Furies wait beyond.

Casella

Test of the poet is knowledge of love,
For Eros is older than Saturn or Jove;
Never was poet, of late or of yore,
Who was not tremulous with love-lore.

Shakspeare

I see all human wits
Are measured but a few,
Unmeasured still my Shakspeare sits,
Lone as the blessed Jew.

Hafiz

Her passions the shy violet
From Hafiz never hides;
Love-longings of the raptured bird
The bird to him confides.

Nature in Leasts

As sings the pine-tree in the wind,
So sings in the wind a sprig of the pine;
Her strength and soul has laughing France
Shed in each drop of wine.

ʹΑΔΑΚΡΥΝ ΝΕΜΟΝΤΑΙ ΑΙΩΝΑ

'A new commandment,' said the smiling Muse,
'I give my darling son, Thou shalt not preach'; –
Luther, Fox, Behmen, Swedenborg, grew pale,
And, on the instant, rosier clouds upbore
Hafiz and Shakspeare with their shining choirs.

From
SELECTED POEMS
(1876)

THE NUN'S ASPIRATION

The yesterday doth never smile,
To-day goes drudging through the while,
Yet in the name of Godhead, I
The morrow front, and can defy;
Though I am weak, yet God, when prayed,
Cannot withhold his conquering aid.
Ah me! it was my childhood's thought,
If He should make my web a blot
On life's fair picture of delight,
My heart's content would find it right.
But O, these waves and leaves, –
When haply stoic Nature grieves, –
No human speech so beautiful
As their murmurs mine to lull.
On this altar God hath built
I lay my vanity and guilt;
Nor me can Hope or Passion urge
Hearing as now the lofty dirge
Which blasts of Northern mountains hymn,
Nature's funeral, high and dim, –
Sable pageantry of clouds,
Mourning summer laid in shrouds.
Many a day shall dawn and die,
Many an angel wander by,
And passing, light my sunken turf

Moist perhaps by ocean surf,
Forgotten amid splendid tombs,
Yet wreathed and hid by summer blooms.
On earth I dream; – I die to be:
Time! shake not thy bald head at me.
I challenge thee to hurry past,
Or for my turn to fly too fast.
Think me not numbed or halt with age,
Or cares that earth to earth engage,
Caught with love's cord of twisted beams,
Or mired by climate's gross extremes.
I tire of shams, I rush to Be,
I pass with yonder comet free, –
Pass with the comet into space
Which mocks thy æons to embrace;
Æons which tardily unfold
Realm beyond realm, – extent untold;
No early morn, no evening late, –
Realms self-upheld, disdaining Fate,
Whose shining sons, too great for fame,
Never heard thy weary name;
Nor lives the tragic bard to say
How drear the part I held in one,
How lame the other limped away.

HYMN

Sung at the Second Church, Boston, at the
Ordination of Rev. Chandler Robbins

We love the venerable house
   Our fathers built to God; –
In heaven are kept their grateful vows,
   Their dust endears the sod.

Here holy thoughts a light have shed
   From many a radiant face,
And prayers of humble virtue made
   The perfume of the place.

And anxious hearts have pondered here
   The mystery of life,
And prayed the eternal Light to clear
   Their doubts, and aid their strife.

From humble tenements around
   Came up the pensive train,
And in the church a blessing found
   That filled their homes again;

For faith and peace and mighty love
   That from the Godhead flow,
Showed them the life of Heaven above
   Springs from the life below.

143

They live with God; their homes are dust;
  Yet here their children pray,
And in this fleeting lifetime trust
  To find the narrow way.

On him who by the altar stands,
  On him thy blessing fall,
Speak through his lips thy pure commands,
  Thou heart that lovest all.

CUPIDO

The solid, solid universe
Is pervious to Love;
With bandaged eyes he never errs,
Around, below, above.
His blinding light
He flingeth white
On God's and Satan's brood,
And reconciles
By mystic wiles
The evil and the good.

BOSTON
Sicut patribus, sit Deus nobis

Read in Faneuil Hall, on December 16, 1873, on the
Centennial Anniversary of the Destruction of the Tea
in Boston Harbor

The rocky nook with hill-tops three
   Looked eastward from the farms,
And twice each day the flowing sea
   Took Boston in its arms;
      The men of yore were stout and poor,
      And sailed for bread to every shore.

And where they went on trade intent
   They did what freemen can,
Their dauntless ways did all men praise,
   The merchant was a man.
      The world was made for honest trade, –
      To plant and eat be none afraid.

The waves that rocked them on the deep
   To them their secret told;
Said the winds that sung the lads to sleep,
   'Like us be free and bold!'
      The honest waves refuse to slaves
      The empire of the ocean caves.

Old Europe groans with palaces,
    Has lords enough and more; –
We plant and build by foaming seas
    A city of the poor; –
        For day by day could Boston Bay
        Their honest labor overpay.

We grant no dukedoms to the few,
    We hold like rights and shall; –
Equal on Sunday in the pew,
    On Monday in the mall.
        For what avail the plough or sail,
        Or land or life, if freedom fail?

The noble craftsman we promote,
    Disown the knave and fool;
Each honest man shall have his vote,
    Each child shall have his school.
        A union then of honest men,
        Or union nevermore again.

The wild rose and the barberry thorn
    Hung out their summer pride
Where now on heated pavements worn
    The feet of millions stride.

Fair rose the planted hills behind
    The good town on the bay,
And where the western hills declined
    The prairie stretched away.

What care though rival cities soar
    Along the stormy coast,
Penn's town, New York, and Baltimore,
    If Boston knew the most!

They laughed to know the world so wide;
    The mountains said, 'Good day!
We greet you well, you Saxon men,
    Up with your towns and stay!'
        The world was made for honest trade, –
        To plant and eat be none afraid.

'For you,' they said, 'no barriers be,
    For you no sluggard rest;
Each street leads downward to the sea,
    Or landward to the West.'

O happy town beside the sea,
    Whose roads lead everywhere to all;
Than thine no deeper moat can be,
    No stouter fence, no steeper wall!

Bad news from George on the English throne:
   'You are thriving well,' said he;
'Now by these presents be it known,
    You shall pay us a tax on tea;
      'T is very small, – no load at all, –
      Honor enough that we send the call.'

'Not so,' said Boston, 'good my lord,
   We pay your governors here
Abundant for their bed and board,
   Six thousand pounds a year.
(Your Highness knows our homely word,)
      Millions for self-government
      But for tribute never a cent.'

The cargo came! and who could blame
   If *Indians* seized the tea,
And, chest by chest, let down the same
   Into the laughing sea?
      For what avail the plough or sail,
      Or land or life, if freedom fail?

The townsmen braved the English king,
   Found friendship in the French,
And Honor joined the patriot ring
   Low on their wooden bench.

O bounteous seas that never fail!
  O day remembered yet!
O happy port that spied the sail
  Which wafted Lafayette!
    Pole-star of light in Europe's night,
    That never faltered from the right.

Kings shook with fear, old empires crave
  The secret force to find
Which fired the little State to save
  The rights of all mankind.

But right is might through all the world;
  Province to province faithful clung,
Through good and ill the war-bolt hurled,
  Till Freedom cheered and the joy-bells rung.

The sea returning day by day
  Restores the world-wide mart;
So let each dweller on the Bay
  Fold Boston in his heart,
    Till these echoes be choked with snows,
    Or over the town blue ocean flows.

Let the blood of her hundred thousands
  Throb in each manly vein;
And the wit of all her wisest,

Make sunshine in her brain.
　　For you can teach the lightning speech,
　　And round the globe your voices reach.

And each shall care for other,
　　And each to each shall bend,
To the poor a noble brother,
　　To the good an equal friend.

A blessing through the ages thus
　　Shield all thy roofs and towers!
God with the fathers, so with us,
　　Thou darling town of ours!

SILENCE

They put their finger on their lip, –
　　The Powers above;
The seas their islands clip,
The moons in Ocean dip, –
　　They love but name not love.

THE THREE DIMENSIONS

'Room for the spheres!' – then first they shined,
And dived into the ample sky;
'Room! room!' cried the new mankind,
And took the oath of liberty.
Room! room! willed the opening mind,
And found it in Variety.

MOTTO TO 'THE POET'

A moody child and wildly wise
Pursued the game with joyful eyes,
Which chose, like meteors, their way,
And rived the dark with private ray:
They overleapt the horizon's edge,
Searched with Apollo's privilege;
Through man, and woman, and sea, and star,
Saw the dance of nature forward far;
Through worlds, and races, and terms, and times,
Saw musical order, and pairing rhymes.

MOTTO TO 'GIFTS'

Gifts of one who loved me, –
'T was high time they came;
When he ceased to love me,
Time they stopped for shame.

MOTTO TO 'NATURE'

The rounded world is fair to see,
Nine times folded in mystery:
Though baffled seers cannot impart
The secret of its laboring heart,
Throb thine with Nature's throbbing breast,
And all is clear from east to west.
Spirit that lurks each form within
Beckons to spirit of its kin;
Self-kindled every atom glows,
And hints the future which it owes.

MOTTO TO 'NOMINALIST AND REALIST'

In countless upward-striving waves
The moon-drawn tide-wave strives;
In thousand far-transplanted grafts
The parent fruit survives;
So, in the new-born millions,
The perfect Adam lives.
Not less are summer-mornings dear
To every child they wake,
And each with novel life his sphere
Fills for his proper sake.

MOTTO TO 'HISTORY'

There is no great and no small
To the Soul that maketh all:
And where it cometh, all things are;
And it cometh everywhere.

SOUTH WIND

In the turbulent beauty
Of a gusty autumn day,
Poet in a wood-crowned headland
Sighed his soul away.
Farms the sunny landscape dappled,
Swan-down clouds dappled the farms,
Cattle lowed in hazy distance
Where far oaks outstretched their arms.
Sudden gusts came full of meaning,
All too much to him they said; –
Southwinds have long memories,
Of that be none afraid.
I cannot tell rude listeners
Half the telltale Southwind said,
'Twould bring the blushes of yon maples
To a man and to a maid.

From
THE UNPUBLISHED POEMS

William does thy frigid soul,
The charms of poetry deny,
And think thy heart beyond controul,
Of each Parnassian Deity?

This I suspect from that cold look,
Quenching like ice Apollo's fire,
With which each vagrant verse you took,
When offer'd from my humble lyre.

Not that in truth I mean to say,
I ever had a lyre – not I –
Rhymers you know have got a way,
To Tell a *bumper*, alias *lie*. –

– I love quotations – Dr Gibbs –
Or some one else perhaps – has said,
– Poets have leave to publish fibs,
And 't is a portion of their trade –

But to return – 't is wrong to say,
That I should not have leave to write,
My maxim is – write while it's day, –
For soon, forsooth it will be night,

That is – poor Ralph must versify,
Through College *like a thousand drums*
But when well *through* then then oh my
The dark dull *night* of Business comes.

While this my letter you peruse,
Frown no long-faced *apostrophe*,
Dare not to blame the wayward muse,
Nor scowl the *scrof'lous* brow at me –

* * *

Perhaps thy lot in life is higher
   Than the fates assign to me
While they fulfil thy large desire
   And bid my hopes as visions flee
But grant me still in joy or sorrow
   In grief or hope to claim thy heart
And I will then defy the morrow
   Whilst I fulfil a loyal part.

SONG
Tune 'Scots wha hae wi' Wallace bled'

Shout for those whose course is done, –
Bow you to their setting sun,
– Souls of patriots who won
                    Noble Liberty.

Fell Britannia's tyrant power
Quailed in combat's fearful hour;
Lowly did the Lion cower
                    To their victory.

Stars of Freedom's spangled banner!
Burst ye forth in loud hosanna,
While the morning breezes fan her
                    Passing cheerfully.

Celebrate with song today,
Feats of eras far away
Ruin to the British sway
                    O'er Columbia

*   *   *

I spread my gorgeous sail
Upon a starless sea
And o'er the deep with a chilly gale
My painted bark sailed fast & free –

Old Ocean shook his waves
Beneath the roaring wind,
But the little keel of the mariner braves
The foaming abyss, & the midnight blind.

The firmament darkened overhead,
Below, the surges swelled, –
My bark ran low in the watery bed,
As the tempest breath its course compelled.

I took my silver lyre,
And waked its voice on high; –
The wild blasts were hushed to admire,
And the stars looked out from the charmed sky.

Bear me then, ye wild waters,
To Apollo's Delphian isle,
My name is *Music*, in Castalie known,
Where bowers of joy the Nine beguile. –

*   *   *

O what is Heaven but the fellowship
Of minds that each can stand against the world,
By its own meek but incorruptible will?

* * *

Ah strange strange strange
The Dualism of man –
That he can enlist
But half his being in his act.

* * *

See yonder leafless trees against the sky,
How they diffuse themselves into the air,
And ever subdividing separate,
Limbs into branches, branches into twigs,
As if they loved the element, & hasted
To dissipate their being into it.

* * *

Do that which you can do
The world will feel its need of you.

* * *

Few are free
All might be
'T is the height
Of the soul's flight

*   *   *

Van Buren

The towers that generations did combine
To build & grace, a rat may undermine.

*   *   *

The Future

How many big events to shake the earth,
Lie packed in silence waiting for their birth.

*   *   *

Rex

The bard & mystic held me for their own
I filled the dream of sad poetic maids
I took the friendly noble by the hand
I was the trustee of the handcartman
The brother of the fisher, porter, swain, –
And these from the crowd's edge well pleased beheld
The honor done to me as done to them.

*   *   *

And when I am entombed in my place,
Be it remembered of a single man,
He never, though he dearly loved his race,
For fear of human eyes, swerved from his plan.

*   *   *

Bard or dunce is blest, but hard
Is it to be half a bard.

* * *

It takes philosopher or fool
To build a fire or keep a school.

* * *

Tell men what they knew before
Paint the prospect from their door.

* * *

I use the knife
To save the life.

* * *

There is no evil but can speak,
If the wheel want oil 't will creak.

* * *

The sea reflects the rosy sky,
The sky doth marry the blue main.

* * *

In this sour world, O summerwind
Who taught thee sweet to blow
Who should not love me, summerwind,
If thou canst flatter so

*   *   *

Look danger in the eye it vanishes
Anatomize that roaring populace
Big dire & overwhelming as they seem
Piecemeal 't is nothing. Some of them scream
Fearing the others some are lookers on
One of them hectic day by day consumes
And one will die tomorrow of the flux
One of them has already changed his mind
And falls out with the ringleader and one
Has seen his creditor amidst the crowd
And flees. And there are heavy eyes
That miss their sleep & meditate retreat.
A few malignant heads keep up the din
The rest are idle boys.

*   *   *

As I walked in the wood
The silence into music broke
Sang the thrush in the dark oak
I unwilling to intrude
Slink into nigh solitude
Till warned by a scout of a jay
That flying courier so gay
That he sees me if I see not him
His eyes are bright if mine are dim

* * *

I sat upon the ground
I leaned against an ancient pine
The pleasant breeze
Shook the forest tops like waves of ocean
I felt of the trunk the gentle motion

* * *

Good Charles the spring's adorer
True worshipper of Flora
Know'st thou the gay Rhodora
 That blossoms in the May?
It blooms in dark nooks
By the wood loving brooks
 And makes their twilight gay.

* * *

Around the man who seeks a noble end
Not angels but divinities attend.

* * *

In the deep heart of man a poet dwells
Who all the day of life his summer story tells
Scatters on every eye dust of his spells
Scent form & color to the flowers & shells
Wins the believing child with wondrous tales

Touches a cheek with colors of romance
And crowds a history into a glance
Gives beauty to the lake & fountain
Spies over sea the fires of the mountain
When thrushes ope their throat, 't is he that sings
And he that paints the oriole's fiery wings
The little Shakspeare in the maiden's heart
Makes Romeo of a ploughboy on his cart
Opens the eye to Virtue's starlike meed
And gives persuasion to a gentle deed.

* * *

O what are heroes prophets men
But pipes through which the breath of Pan doth blow
A momentary music. Being's tide
Swells hitherward & myriads of forms
Live, robed with beauty, painted by the Sun:
Their dust pervaded by the nerves of God
Throbs with an overmastering energy
Knowing & doing. Ebbs the tide, they lie
White hollow shells upon the desart shore.
But not the less the eternal wave rolls on
To animate new millions, & exhale
Races & planets its enchanted foam.

* * *

Yet sometime to the sorrow stricken
Shall his own sorrow seem impertinent
A thing that takes no more root in the world
Than doth the traveller's shadow on the rock

* * *

The Bohemian Hymn

In many forms we try
To utter God's infinity
But the boundless hath no form
And the Universal Friend
Doth as far transcend
An angel as a worm.

The great Idea baffles wit
Language falters under it
It leaves the learned in the lurch
Nor art nor power nor toil can find
The measure of the eternal Mind
Nor hymn nor prayer nor church.

* * *

Kind & holy were the words —
O how trustingly they fell!
Music wants such sweet accords —
Sister, this thy perfect spell.

All the woman now was dropt,
All the friend came forth to me,
The beauty I had pictured oft
Was vanished utterly
Before the dearer emanation
Of undefiled affection,
Of earnest, wistful, ancient love,
With clear & liquid eye,
Older than the gods above,
Fountain of their deity.
Yet thou showed me no love
For the sake of love,
That for meaner souls was made
To whom passion is their bread.
Thou didst wrap thy love in thought
It to me in wisdom taught
In the rapid utterance
Of thy noble aim & hope
In the clear deliverance
Of the will's & wisdom's scope.
Now pleasant fall the blinding snows,
And gay to me the darkest night,
A merry catch the cold wind blows,
And Pain can yield its own delight,
Whilst thou to me & I to thee belong
By the high kin of thought, O Sister of my song!

* * *

Divine Inviters! I accept
The courtesy ye have shown & kept
From ancient ages for the bard,
To modulate
With finer fate
A fortune harsh & hard.
With aim like yours
I watch your course,
Who never break your lawful dance
By error or intemperance.
O birds of ether without wings!
O heavenly ships without a sail!
O fire of fire! O best of things!
O mariners who never fail!
Sail swiftly through your amber vault
An animated law, a presence to exalt

*   *   *

Go if thou wilt ambrosial Flower
Go match thee with thy seeming peers
I will wait Heaven's perfect hour
Through the innumerable years

*   *   *

In Walden wood the chickadee
Runs round the pine & maple tree,
Intent on insect slaughter:
O tufted entomologist!
Devour as many as you list,
Then drink in Walden Water.

*   *   *

    Star seer Copernicus
    Only could earn a curse
    A slip of a fellow to show men the stars
    What a scandalous slip of a fellow was he
    Presuming to show what men wished not to see
Misunderstood – Misunderstood
How dared the old graybeard be misunderstood

*   *   *

At last the poet spoke
The richest gifts are vain
As lightning in yon dark clouds' grain
A poison in the world's veins creeps
A devil in celestial deeps

*   *   *

170

I grieve that better souls than mine
Docile read my measured line
High destined youths & holy maids
Hallow these my orchard shades
Environ me & me baptize
With light that streams from gracious eyes,
I dare not be beloved or known,
I ungrateful, I alone.

* * *

Nantasket

Lobster-car, boat, or fishbasket,
Peeps, noddies, oldsquaws, or quail,
To Musketaquid what from Nantasket,
What token of greeting & hail?

Can we tie up & send you our thunder, –
Pulse-beat of the sea on the shore?
Or our Rainbow, the daughter of Wonder,
Our rock Massasoit's palace-door.

White pebbles from Nantasket beach,
Whereon to write the maiden's name;
Shells, sea-eggs, sea flowers, could they teach
Thee the fair haunts from whence they came!

* * *

Water

The Water understands
Civilization well –
It wets my foot, but prettily,
It chills my life, but wittily,
It is not disconcerted,
It is not broken-hearted,
Well used, it decketh joy,
Adorneth, doubleth joy;
Ill-used it will destroy
In perfect time and measure,
With a face of golden pleasure,
Elegantly destroy.

* * *

Where the fungus broad & red
Lifts its head
Like poisoned loaf of elfin bread
Where the aster grew
With the social goldenrod
In a chapel which the dew
Made beautiful for God
The maple street
In the houseless wood
O what would nature say
She spared no speech today

The fungus & the bulrush spoke
Answered the pinetree & the oak
The wizard South blew down the glen
Filled the straits & filled the wide,
Each maple leaf turned up its silver side.
All things shine in his damp ray
And all we see are pictures high
Many a high hill side
Which oaks of pride
Climb to their tops
And boys run out upon their leafy ropes

In the houseless wood
Voices followed after
Every shrub & grapeleaf
Rang with fairy laughter
I have heard them fall
Like the strain of all
King Oberon's minstrelsy
    Would hear the everlasting
And know the only strong
You must worship fasting
You must listen long
Words of the air
Which birds of the air
Carry aloft below around
To the isles of the deep

To the snow-capped steep
To the thundercloud
To the loud bazaar
To the haram of Caliph & Kremlin of Czar
Is the verse original
Let its numbers rise & fall
As the winds do when they call
One to another

Come search the wood for flowers
Wild tea & wild pea
Grape vine & succory
Coreopsis
And liatris
Flaunting in their bowers
Grass with greenflag halfmast high
Succory to match the sky
Columbine with horn of honey
Scented fern & agrimony
Forest full of essences
Fit for fairy presences,
Peppermint & sassafras
Sweet fern, mint, & vernal grass,
Panax, black birch, sugar maple,
Sweet & scent for Dian's table,
Elder-blow, sarsaparilla,
Wild-rose, lily, dry vanilla.

* * *

From the stores of eldest Matter
The deep-eyed flame obedient water
Transparent air all-feeding earth
He took the flower of all their worth
And best with best in sweet consent
Combined a new temperament.

* * *

And the best gift of God
Is the love of superior souls

* * *

Stout Sparta shrined the god of Laughter
In a niche below the rafter,
Visible from every seat
Where the young men carve their meat.

* * *

Brother, no decrepitude
Cramps the limbs of Time;
As fleet his feet, his hands as good,
His vision as sublime.
As when at first Jehovah hurled
The Sun & each revolving world.

* * *

Who knows this or that
Hark in the wall to the rat
Since the world was, he has gnawed;
Of his wisdom of his fraud
What dost thou know
In the wretched little beast
Is life & heart
Child & parent
Not without relation
To fruitful field & sun & moon
What art thou? his wicked eye
Is cruel to thy cruelty.

* * *

Saadi loved the new & old
The near & far the town & wold –
Him when Genius urged to roam
Stronger Custom brot him home

* * *

And as the light divided the dark
Thorough with living swords
So shalt thou pierce the distant age
With adamantine words.

* * *

When devils bite
A damned parasite
Strikes at their throat & stings them home

*　*　*

Comfort with a purring cat
Prosperity in a white hat

*　*　*

I cannot find a place so lonely
To harbour thee & me only
I cannot find a nook so deep
So sheltered may suffice to keep
The ever glowing festival
When thou & I to each are all

*　*　*

This shining hour is an edifice
Which the Omnipotent cannot rebuild

*　*　*

The sparrow is rich in her nest
The bee has her desire
The lover in his love is blest
The poet in his brain of fire

*　*　*

Bended to fops who bent to him
Surface with surfaces did swim
And in the fashionable crowd
None more obsequious heartless bowed
'Sorrow! Sorrow!' the Angels cried
'Is this dear nature's manly pride!
Call hither thy mortal enemy
Make him glad thy fall to see.'

*   *   *

Elizabeth Hoar

Almost I am tempted to essay
For sympathetic eyes the portraiture
Of the good angels that environ me.
My sister is a Greek in mind & face
And well embodies to these latest years
The truth of those high sculptors old who drew
In marble or in bronze, on vase or frieze
The perfect forms of Pallas or the Muse;
Forms in simplicity complete
And beauty of the soul disdaining art.
So bright, so positive, so much itself,
Yet so adapted to the work it wrought
It drew true love, but was complete alone.
She seemed to commune with herself, & say,
I cannot stoop to custom & the crowd,

For either I will marry with a star,
Or I will pick threads in a factory.
So perfect in her action, one would say,
She condescended if she added speech.
Her look was sympathy, & though she spoke
Better than all the rest, she did not speak
Worthy of her. She read in many books,
And loved the Greek as 't were her mother tongue
She knew the value of the passing day
Thought it no mark of virtue to be scornful
Or cry for better company, but held
Each day a solid good; never mistook
The fashionable judgment for her own.
So keen perception that no judge or scribe
Could vie with her unerring estimate.
When through much silence & delay she spoke,
It was the Mind's own oracle, through joy
And love of truth or beauty so perceived:
Never a poor return on self.

* * *

Cloud upon cloud
The world is a seeming,
Feigns dying, but dies not,
Corpses rise ruddy,
Follow their funerals.
Seest thou not brother

Drops hate detachment,
And atoms disorder,
How they run into plants,
And grow into beauties.
The darkness will glow,
The solitude sing

*   *   *

Since the devil hopping on
From bush to vine from man to dame
Marshals temptations
A million deep
And ever new beauties rise
And with what faults soever
The stock of illusion
Is inexhaustible
I meantime depreciate
Every hour in the market
But the wares I would buy
Are enhanced every hour
I see no other way
Than to run violently from the market

*   *   *

Poets are colorpots
Dovesnecks & opaline
Exquisite daintiness
Vapors of wine
Delicate gloom
Barrel of opium
Blowing simoom
Cloud-collecting, dissipating
Brain relaxing enervating
Put your body on your word
Man & sonnet at accord
Set your foot upon the scales
My foot weighs just a pound
Said the cruel Yankee captain
Trucking for his precious bales
Of ermine skin & silver fur
With the painted islander.

* * *

Thanks to those who go & come
Bringing Hellas, Thebes, & Rome,
As near to me as is my home:
Careful husbands of the mind
Who keep decaying history good,
And do not suffer Tyre or Troy
To know decrepitude.

* * *

I must not borrow light
From history trite
But from friends whom God gave
And the destiny I have

* * *

Comrade of the snow & wind
He left each civil scale behind
Him woodgods fed with honey wild
And of his memory beguiled
In caves & hollow trees he crept
And near the wolf & panther slept
He came to the green ocean's rim
And saw the sea birds skim
Summer & winter o'er the wave
Like creatures made of skiey mould
Impassible to heat or cold.
He stood beside the main
Beautiful but insane
He felt himself as if the sky walked
Or the son of the wind
There was no man near
To mete himself withal

* * *

God only knew how Saadi dined
Roses he ate, & drank the wind

* * *

Friends to me are frozen wine
I wait the sun shall on them shine

* * *

That each should in his house abide,
Therefore was the world so wide

* * *

New England Capitalist

What are his machines
Of steel, brass, leather, oak, & ivory,
But manikins & miniatures,
Dwarfs of one faculty, measured from him,
As nimbly he applies his bending self
Unto the changing world, thus making that
Another weapon of his conquering will?
He built the mills, & by his polities, made
The arms of millions turn them.

Stalwart New Hampshire, mother of men,
Sea-dented Maine, reluctant Carolina,
Must drag his coach, & by arts of peace
He, in the plenitude of love & honor,
Eats up the poor, – poor citizen poor state.
Much has he done,

Has made his telegraph,
Propeller, car, post-office, phototype,
His coast survey, vote by majority,
His life assurance, & star registry,
Preludes & hints of what he meditates; –
Now let him make a harp!

      * * *

  On a raisin stone
The wheels of nature turn,
Out of it the fury comes
Wherewith the spondyls burn.
And, because the seed of the vine
Is creation's heart,
Wash with wine those eyes of thine
To know the hidden part.
Wine is translated wit,
Wine is the day of day,
Wine from the veiled secret
Tears the veil away.

      * * *

Go out into Nature and plant trees
That when the southwind blows
You shall not be warm in your own limbs
But in ten thousand limbs & ten million leaves
Of your blossoming trees of orchard & forest

   Pale Genius roves alone,
No scout can track his way,
None credits him till he have shown
His diamonds to the day.

Not his the feaster's wine,
Nor land, nor gold, nor power,
By want & pain God screeneth him
Till his elected hour.

Go, speed the stars of Thought
On to their shining goals; –
The sower scatters broad his seed,
The wheat thou strew'st be souls.

* * *

Burn your literary verses.
Give us rather the glib curses
Of the truckmen in the street,
Songs of the forecastle
To the caboose.

* * *

   Intellect
Gravely broods apart on joy,
And truth to tell, amused by pain

185

*   *   *

The civil world will much forgive
To bards who from its maxims live
But if, grown bold, the poet dare
Bend his practice to his prayer,
And, following his mighty heart
Shame the time, & live apart,
Vae solis!
I found this, –
That of goods I could not miss
If I fell within the line,
Once a member, all was mine,
Houses, banquets, gardens, fountains,
Fortune's delectable mountains;
But if I would walk alone,
Was neither cloak nor crumb my own

*   *   *

Mask thy wisdom with delight,
Toy with the bow, yet hit the white.
The lesson which the Muses say
Was sweet to hear & to obey.
He loved to round a verse, & play,
Without remoter hope, or fear,
Or purpose, than to please his ear.
And all the golden summer-time

Rung out the hours with happy rhyme.
Meantime every cunning word
Tribes & ages overheard:
Those idle catches told the laws
Holding nature to her Cause.

* * *

Roomy Eternity
Casts her schemes rarely,
And an aeon allows
For each quality and part
In the multitudinous
And many-chambered heart.

* * *

Terminus

For thought & not praise;
Thought is the wages
For which I sell days,
Will gladly sell ages,
And willing grow old,
Deaf, & dumb, & blind, & cold,
Melting matter into dreams,
Panoramas which I saw
And whatever glows or seems
Into substance into Law

* * *

More sweet than my refrain
Was the first drop of April rain

* * *

O Boston city lecture-hearing,
O unitarian God-fearing,
But more, I fear, bad men-revering;
Too civil by half, thine evil guest
Makes thee his byword & his jest,
And scorns the men that honeyed the pest,
Piso & Atticus, with the rest.
Thy fault is much civility,
Thy bane, respectability.
And thou hadst been as wise, & wiser,
Lacking the Daily Advertiser.
Ah, gentlemen, – for you are gentle, –
And mental maids, not sentimental.

* * *

A patch of meadow & upland
Reached by a mile of road,
Soothed by the voice of waters,
With birds & flowers bestowed.

This is my book of Chronicles,
Code, Psalter, lexicon,
My Genesis & calendar
I read it as I run.

It is my consolation
In mild or poignant grief,
My park & my gymnasium,
My out-of-door relief.

I come to it for strength,
Which it can well supply,
For Love draws might from terrene force
And potences of sky.

The tremulous battery, earth,
Responds to touch of man,
It thrills to the antipodes,
From Boston to Japan.

The planets' child the planet knows
And to his joy replies;
To the lark's trill unfolds the rose,
Clouds flush their gayest dyes.

When Ali prayed & loved
Where Syrian waters roll,

Upward the ninth heaven thrilled & moved
At the tread of the jubilant soul.

*   *   *

And he like me is not too proud
To be the poet of the crowd

*   *   *

Parks & ponds are good by day,
But where's the husband doth delight
In black acres of the night?
Not my unseasoned step disturbs
The sleeps of trees or dreams of herbs

*   *   *

For Lyra yet shall be the pole
And grass grow in the Capitol

*   *   *

A score of airy miles will smooth
Rough Monadnock to a gem.

*   *   *

All things rehearse
The meaning of the universe

*   *   *

    Pedants all,
They would be original;
The mute pebble shames their wit,
The echo is ironical
And wiser silence swallows speech.

*   *   *

I leave the book, I leave the wine,
I breathe freer by the pine:
In houses, I am low & mean,
Mountain waters wash me clean,
And by the seawaves I am strong,
I hear their medicinal song,
No balsam but the breeze I crave,
And no physician but the wave.

*   *   *

Easy to match what others do,
Perform the feat as well as they;
Hard to outdo the wise, the true,
And find a loftier way.
The school decays, the learning spoils,
Because of the sons of wine: —
How snatch the stripling from their toils?
Yet can one ray of truth divine
The banquet's blaze outshine.

*   *   *

If wishes would carry me over the land,
I would ride with free bridle today,
I would greet every tree with a grasp of my hand,
I would drink of each river, & swim in each bay.

* * *

Maia

Illusion works impenetrable,
Weaving webs innumerable,
Her gay pictures never fail,
Crowds each on other, veil on veil,
Charmer who will be believed
By Man who thirsts to be deceived.

* * *

Seyd planted where the deluge ploughed,
His hired hands were wind & cloud
His eyes could spy the gods concealed
In each hummock of the field

* * *

Forbore the ant hill, shunned to tread,
In mercy, on one little head

* * *

Borrow Urania's subtile wings
Chasing with words fast-flowing things:
Cling to the sacred fact, nor try
To plant thy shrivelled pedantry
On the shoulders of the sky.

*   *   *

The comrade or the book is good
That puts me in a working mood:
Unless to thought be added will,
Apollo is an imbecile.
What parts, what truth, what fancies shine!
– Ah! but I miss the just design.

*   *   *

Is the pace of nature slow?
Why not from strength to strength
From miracle to miracle
And not as now with retardation
As with sprained foot

*   *   *

Why honor the new men
Who never understood the old

*   *   *

Think not the gods receive thy prayer
In ear & heart, but find it there.

*   *   *

Inspired we must forget our books,
To see the landscape's royal looks.

*   *   *

Upon a rock yet uncreate
Amid a Chaos inchoate
An uncreated being sate
Beneath him rock
Above him cloud
And the cloud was rock
And the rock was cloud
The rock then growing soft & warm
The cloud began to take a form
A form chaotic vast & vague
Which issued in the cosmic egg
Then the being uncreate
Upon the egg did incubate
And thus became an incubator
And of the egg did allegate
And thus became an alligator
And the incubate was potentate
But the alligator was potentator

LONGER POEMS

WOODNOTES I

1.

For this present, hard
Is the fortune of the bard,
   Born out of time;
All his accomplishment,
From Nature's utmost treasure spent,
   Booteth not him.
When the pine tosses its cones
To the song of its waterfall tones,
He speeds to the woodland walks,
To birds and trees he talks:
Cæsar of his leafy Rome,
There the poet is at home.
He goes to the river-side, –
Not hook nor line hath he;
He stands in the meadows wide, –
Nor gun nor scythe to see;
With none has he to do,
And none seek him,
Nor men below,
Nor spirits dim.
Sure some god his eye enchants:
What he knows nobody wants.
In the wood he travels glad,

Without better fortune had,
Melancholy without bad.
Planter of celestial plants,
What he knows nobody wants;
What he knows he hides, not vaunts.
Knowledge this man prizes best
Seems fantastic to the rest:
Pondering shadows, colors, clouds,
Grass-buds, and caterpillar-shrouds,
Boughs on which the wild bees settle,
Tints that spot the violets' petal,
Why Nature loves the number five,
And why the star-form she repeats:
Lover of all things alive,
Wonderer at all he meets,
Wonderer chiefly at himself, –
Who can tell him what he is?
Or how meet in human elf
Coming and past eternities?

2.

And such I knew, a forest seer,
A minstrel of the natural year,
Foreteller of the vernal ides,
Wise harbinger of spheres and tides,
A lover true, who knew by heart

Each joy the mountain dales impart;
It seemed that Nature could not raise
A plant in any secret place,
In quaking bog, on snowy hill,
Beneath the grass that shades the rill,
Under the snow, between the rocks,
In damp fields known to bird and fox,
But he would come in the very hour
It opened in its virgin bower,
As if a sunbeam showed the place,
And tell its long-descended race.
It seemed as if the breezes brought him;
It seemed as if the sparrows taught him;
As if by secret sight he knew
Where, in far fields, the orchis grew.
Many haps fall in the field
Seldom seen by wishful eyes,
But all her shows did Nature yield,
To please and win this pilgrim wise.
He saw the partridge drum in the woods;
He heard the woodcock's evening hymn;
He found the tawny thrush's broods;
And the shy hawk did wait for him;
What others did at distance hear,
And guessed within the thicket's gloom,
Was showed to this philosopher,
And at his bidding seemed to come.

3.

In unploughed Maine he sought the lumberers' gang,
Where from a hundred lakes young rivers sprang;
He trode the unplanted forest floor, whereon
The all-seeing sun for ages hath not shone;
Where feeds the moose, and walks the surly bear,
And up the tall mast runs the woodpecker.
He saw beneath dim aisles, in odorous beds,
The slight Linnæa hang its twin-born heads,
And blessed the monument of the man of flowers,
Which breathes his sweet fame through the
    northern bowers.
He heard, when in the grove, at intervals,
With sudden roar the aged pine-tree falls, –
One crash, the death-hymn of the perfect tree,
Declares the close of its green century.
Low lies the plant to whose creation went
Sweet influence from every element;
Whose living towers the years conspired to build,
Whose giddy top the morning loved to gild.
Through these green tents, by eldest Nature dressed,
He roamed, content alike with man and beast.
Where darkness found him he lay glad at night;
There the red morning touched him with its light.
Three moons his great heart him a hermit made,
So long he roved at will the boundless shade.
The timid it concerns to ask their way,

And fear what foe in caves and swamps can stray,
To make no step until the event is known,
And ills to come as evils past bemoan.
Not so the wise; no coward watch he keeps
To spy what danger on his pathway creeps;
Go where he will, the wise man is at home,
His hearth the earth, – his hall the azure dome;
Where his clear spirit leads him, there's his road,
By God's own light illumined and foreshowed.

4.

'Twas one of the charmed days,
When the genius of God doth flow,
The wind may alter twenty ways,
A tempest cannot blow;
It may blow north, it still is warm;
Or south, it still is clear;
Or east, it smells like a clover-farm;
Or west, no thunder fear.
The musing peasant lowly great
Beside the forest water sate;
The rope-like pine roots crosswise grown
Composed the network of his throne;
The wide lake, edged with sand and grass,
Was burnished to a floor of glass,
Painted with shadows green and proud
Of the tree and of the cloud.

He was the heart of all the scene;
On him the sun looked more serene;
To hill and cloud his face was known, –
It seemed the likeness of their own;
They knew by secret sympathy
The public child of earth and sky.
'You ask,' he said, 'what guide
Me through trackless thickets led,
Through thick-stemmed woodlands rough and wide?
I found the water's bed.
The watercourses were my guide;
I travelled grateful by their side,
Or through their channel dry;
They led me through the thicket damp,
Through brake and fern, the beavers' camp,
Through beds of granite cut my road,
And their resistless friendship showed;
The falling waters led me,
The foodful waters fed me,
And brought me to the lowest land,
Unerring to the ocean sand.
The moss upon the forest bark
Was polestar when the night was dark;
The purple berries in the wood
Supplied me necessary food;
For Nature ever faithful is
To such as trust her faithfulness.

When the forest shall mislead me,
When the night and morning lie,
When sea and land refuse to feed me,
'Twill be time enough to die;
Then will yet my mother yield
A pillow in her greenest field,
Nor the June flowers scorn to cover
The clay of their departed lover.'

MAY-DAY

Daughter of Heaven and Earth, coy Spring,
With sudden passion languishing,
Maketh all things softly smile,
Painteth pictures mile on mile,
Holds a cup with cowslip-wreaths,
Whence a smokeless incense breathes.
Girls are peeling the sweet willow,
Poplar white, and Gilead-tree,
And troops of boys
Shouting with whoop and hilloa,
And hip, hip, three times three.
The air is full of whistlings bland;
What was that I heard
Out of the hazy land?
Harp of the wind, or song of bird,
Or clapping of shepherd's hands,
Or vagrant booming of the air,
Voice of a meteor lost in day?
Such tidings of the starry sphere
Can this elastic air convey.
Or haply 't was the cannonade
Of the pent and darkened lake,
Cooled by the pendent mountain's shade,
Whose deeps, till beams of noonday break,
Afflicted moan, and latest hold

Even into May the iceberg cold.
Was it a squirrel's pettish bark,
Or clarionet of jay? or hark,
Where yon wedged line the Nestor leads,
Steering north with raucous cry
Through tracts and provinces of sky,
Every night alighting down
In new landscapes of romance,
Where darkling feed the clamorous clans
By lonely lakes to men unknown.
Come the tumult whence it will,
Voice of sport, or rush of wings,
It is a sound, it is a token
That the marble sleep is broken,
And a change has passed on things.

  Beneath the calm, within the light,
A hid unruly appetite
Of swifter life, a surer hope,
Strains every sense to larger scope,
Impatient to anticipate
The halting steps of aged Fate.
Slow grows the palm, too slow the pearl:
When Nature falters, fain would zeal
Grasp the felloes of her wheel,

And grasping give the orbs another whirl.
Turn swiftlier round, O tardy ball!
And sun this frozen side,
Bring hither back the robin's call,
Bring back the tulip's pride.

Why chidest thou the tardy Spring?
The hardy bunting does not chide;
The blackbirds make the maples ring
With social cheer and jubilee;
The redwing flutes his *o-ka-lee*,
The robins know the melting snow;
The sparrow meek, prophetic-eyed,
Her nest beside the snow-drift weaves,
Secure the osier yet will hide
Her callow brood in mantling leaves;
And thou, by science all undone,
Why only must thy reason fail
To see the southing of the sun?

As we thaw frozen flesh with snow,
So Spring will not, foolish fond,
Mix polar night with tropic glow,
Nor cloy us with unshaded sun,
Nor wanton skip with bacchic dance,
But she has the temperance
Of the gods, whereof she is one, –

Masks her treasury of heat
Under east-winds crossed with sleet.
Plants and birds and humble creatures
Well accept her rule austere;
Titan-born, to hardy natures
Cold is genial and dear.
As Southern wrath to Northern right
Is but straw to anthracite;
As in the day of sacrifice,
When heroes piled the pyre,
The dismal Massachusetts ice
Burned more than others' fire,
So Spring guards with surface cold
The garnered heat of ages old:
Hers to sow the seed of bread,
That man and all the kinds be fed;
And, when the sunlight fills the hours,
Dissolves the crust, displays the flowers.

The world rolls round, – mistrust it not, –
Befalls again what once befell;
All things return, both sphere and mote,
And I shall hear my bluebird's note,
And dream the dream of Auburn dell.

When late I walked, in earlier days,
All was stiff and stark;
Knee-deep snows choked all the ways,

In the sky no spark;
Firm-braced I sought my ancient woods,
Struggling through the drifted roads;
The whited desert knew me not,
Snow-ridges masked each darling spot;
The summer dells, by genius haunted,
One arctic moon had disenchanted.
All the sweet secrets therein hid
By Fancy, ghastly spells undid.
Eldest mason, Frost, had piled,
With wicked ingenuity,
Swift cathedrals in the wild;
The piny hosts were sheeted ghosts
In the star-lit minster aisled.
I found no joy: the icy wind
Might rule the forest to his mind.
Who would freeze in frozen brakes?
Back to books and sheltered home,
And wood-fire flickering on the walls,
To hear, when, 'mid our talk and games,
Without the baffled north-wind calls.
But soft! a sultry morning breaks;
The cowslips make the brown brook gay;
A happier hour, a longer day.
Now the sun leads in the May,
Now desire of action wakes,
And the wish to roam.

The caged linnet in the spring
Hearkens for the choral glee,
When his fellows on the wing
Migrate from the Southern Sea;
When trellised grapes their flowers unmask,
And the new-born tendrils twine,
The old wine darkling in the cask
Feels the bloom on the living vine,
And bursts the hoops at hint of spring:
And so, perchance, in Adam's race,
Of Eden's bower some dream-like trace
Survived the Flight, and swam the Flood,
And wakes the wish in youngest blood
To tread the forfeit Paradise,
And feed once more the exile's eyes;
And ever when the happy child
In May beholds the blooming wild,
And hears in heaven the bluebird sing,
'Onward,' he cries, 'your baskets bring, –
In the next field is air more mild,
And o'er yon hazy crest is Eden's balmier spring.'

Not for a regiment's parade,
Nor evil laws or rulers made,
Blue Walden rolls its cannonade,
But for a lofty sign
Which the Zodiac threw,

That the bondage-days are told,
And waters free as winds shall flow.
Lo! how all the tribes combine
To rout the flying foe.
See, every patriot oak-leaf throws
His elfin length upon the snows,
Not idle, since the leaf all day
Draws to the spot the solar ray,
Ere sunset quarrying inches down,
And half-way to the mosses brown;
While the grass beneath the rime
Has hints of the propitious time,
And upward pries and perforates
Through the cold slab a thousand gates,
Till green lances peering through
Bend happy in the welkin blue.

April cold with dropping rain
Willows and lilacs brings again,
The whistle of returning birds,
And trumpet-lowing of the herds.
The scarlet maple-keys betray
What potent blood hath modest May;
What fiery force the earth renews,
The wealth of forms, the flush of hues;
Joy shed in rosy waves abroad
Flows from the heart of Love, the Lord.

Hither rolls the storm of heat;
I feel its finer billows beat
Like a sea which me infolds;
Heat with viewless fingers moulds,
Swells, and mellows, and matures,
Paints, and flavors, and allures,
Bird and brier inly warms,
Still enriches and transforms,
Gives the reed and lily length,
Adds to oak and oxen strength,
Boils the world in tepid lakes,
Burns the world, yet burnt remakes;
Enveloping heat, enchanted robe,
Wraps the daisy and the globe,
Transforming what it doth infold,
Life out of death, new out of old,
Painting fawns' and leopards' fells,
Seethes the gulf-encrimsoning shells,
Fires gardens with a joyful blaze
Of tulips, in the morning's rays.
The dead log touched bursts into leaf,
The wheat-blade whispers of the sheaf.
What god is this imperial Heat,
Earth's prime secret, sculpture's seat?
Doth it bear hidden in its heart
Water-line patterns of all art,
All figures, organs, hues, and graces?

Is it Dædalus? is it Love?
Or walks in mask almighty Jove,
And drops from Power's redundant horn
All seeds of beauty to be born?

   Where shall we keep the holiday,
And duly greet the entering May?
Too strait and low our cottage doors,
And all unmeet our carpet floors;
Nor spacious court, nor monarch's hall,
Suffice to hold the festival.
Up and away! where haughty woods
Front the liberated floods:
We will climb the broad-backed hills,
Hear the uproar of their joy;
We will mark the leaps and gleams
Of the new-delivered streams,
And the murmuring rivers of sap
Mount in the pipes of the trees,
Giddy with day, to the topmost spire,
Which for a spike of tender green
Bartered its powdery cap;
And the colors of joy in the bird,
And the love in its carol heard,
Frog and lizard in holiday coats,
And turtle brave in his golden spots;
We will hear the tiny roar

Of the insects evermore,
While cheerful cries of crag and plain
Reply to the thunder of river and main

    As poured the flood of the ancient sea
Spilling over mountain chains,
Bending forests as bends the sedge,
Faster flowing o'er the plains, –
A world-wide wave with a foaming edge
That rims the running silver sheet, –
So pours the deluge of the heat
Broad northward o'er the land,
Painting artless paradises,
Drugging herbs with Syrian spices,
Fanning secret fires which glow
In columbine and clover-blow,
Climbing the northern zones,
Where a thousand pallid towns
Lie like cockles by the main,
Or tented armies on a plain.
The million-handed sculptor moulds
Quaintest bud and blossom folds,
The million-handed painter pours
Opal hues and purple dye;
Azaleas flush the island floors,
And the tints of heaven reply.

Wreaths for the May! for happy Spring
To-day shall all her dowry bring,
The love of kind, the joy, the grace,
Hymen of element and race,
Knowing well to celebrate
With song and hue and star and state,
With tender light and youthful cheer,
The spousals of the new-born year.
Lo Love's inundation poured
Over space and race abroad!

Spring is strong and virtuous,
Broad-sowing, cheerful, plenteous,
Quickening underneath the mould
Grains beyond the price of gold.
So deep and large her bounties are,
That one broad, long midsunmer day
Shall to the planet overpay
The ravage of a year of war.

Drug the cup, thou butler sweet,
And send the nectar round;
The feet that slid so long on sleet
Are glad to feel the ground.
Fill and saturate each kind
With good according to its mind,
Fill each kind and saturate

With good agreeing with its fate,
Willow and violet, maiden and man.

The bitter-sweet, the haunting air
Creepeth, bloweth everywhere;
It preys on all, all prey on it,
Blooms in beauty, thinks in wit,
Stings the strong with enterprise,
Makes travellers long for Indian skies,
And where it comes this courier fleet
Fans in all hearts expectance sweet,
As if to-morrow should redeem
The vanished rose of evening's dream.
By houses lies a fresher green,
On men and maids a ruddier mien,
As if time brought a new relay
Of shining virgins every May,
And Summer came to ripen maids
To a beauty that not fades.

The ground-pines wash their rusty green,
The maple-tops their crimson tint,
On the soft path each track is seen,
The girl's foot leaves its neater print.
The pebble loosened from the frost
Asks of the urchin to be tost.
In flint and marble beats a heart,

The kind Earth takes her children's part,
The green lane is the school-boy's friend,
Low leaves his quarrel apprehend,
The fresh ground loves his top and ball,
The air rings jocund to his call,
The brimming brook invites a leap,
He dives the hollow, climbs the steep.
The youth reads omens where he goes,
And speaks all languages the rose.
The wood-fly mocks with tiny noise
The far halloo of human voice;
The perfumed berry on the spray
Smacks of faint memories far away.
A subtle chain of countless rings
The next unto the farthest brings,
And, striving to be man, the worm
Mounts through all the spires of form.

I saw the bud-crowned Spring go forth,
Stepping daily onward north
To greet staid ancient cavaliers
Filing single in stately train.
And who, and who are the travellers?
They were Night and Day, and Day and Night,
Pilgrims wight with step forthright.
I saw the Days deformed and low,
Short and bent by cold and snow;

The merry Spring threw wreaths on them,
Flower-wreaths gay with bud and bell;
Many a flower and many a gem,
They were refreshed by the smell,
They shook the snow from hats and shoon,
They put their April raiment on;
And those eternal forms,
Unhurt by a thousand storms,
Shot up to the height of the sky again,
And danced as merrily as young men.
I saw them mask their awful glance
Sidewise meek in gossamer lids;
And to speak my thought if none forbids,
It was as if the eternal gods,
Tired of their starry periods,
Hid their majesty in cloth
Woven of tulips and painted moth.
On carpets green the maskers march
Below May's well-appointed arch,
Each star, each god, each grace amain,
Every joy and virtue speed,
Marching duly in her train,
And fainting Nature at her need
Is made whole again.

'T was the vintage-day of field and wood,
When magic wine for bards is brewed;

Every tree and stem and chink
Gushed with syrup to the brink.
The air stole into the streets of towns,
And betrayed the fund of joy
To the high-school and medalled boy:
On from hall to chamber ran,
From youth to maid, from boy to man,
To babes, and to old eyes as well.
'Once more,' the old man cried, 'ye clouds,
Airy turrets purple-piled,
Which once my infancy beguiled,
Beguile me with the wonted spell.
I know ye skilful to convoy
The total freight of hope and joy
Into rude and homely nooks,
Shed mocking lustres on shelf of books,
On farmer's byre, on meadow-pipes,
Or on a pool of dancing chips.
I care not if the pomps you show
Be what they soothfast appear,
Or if yon realms in sunset glow
Be bubbles of the atmosphere.
And if it be to you allowed
To fool me with a shining cloud,
So only new griefs are consoled
By new delights, as old by old,
Frankly I will be your guest,

Count your change and cheer the best.
The world hath overmuch of pain, –
If Nature give me joy again,
Of such deceit I'll not complain.'

Ah! well I mind the calendar,
Faithful through a thousand years,
Of the painted race of flowers,
Exact to days, exact to hours,
Counted on the spacious dial
Yon broidered zodiac girds.
I know the pretty almanac
Of the punctual coming-back,
On their due days, of the birds.
I marked them yestermorn,
A flock of finches darting
Beneath the crystal arch,
Piping, as they flew, a march, –
Belike the one they used in parting
Last year from yon oak or larch;
Dusky sparrows in a crowd,
Diving, darting northward free,
Suddenly betook them all,
Every one to his hole in the wall,
Or to his niche in the apple-tree.
I greet with joy the choral trains
Fresh from palms and Cuba's canes.

Best gems of Nature's cabinet,
With dews of tropic morning wet,
Beloved of children, bards, and Spring,
O birds, your perfect virtues bring,
Your song, your forms, your rhythmic flight,
Your manners for the heart's delight,
Nestle in hedge, or barn, or roof,
Here weave your chamber weather-proof,
Forgive our harms, and condescend
To man, as to a lubber friend,
And, generous, teach his awkward race
Courage, and probity, and grace!

Poets praise that hidden wine
Hid in milk we drew
At the barrier of Time,
When our life was new.
We had eaten fairy fruit,
We were quick from head to foot,
All the forms we looked on shone
As with diamond dews thereon.
What cared we for costly joys,
The Museum's far-fetched toys?
Gleam of sunshine on the wall
Poured a deeper cheer than all
The revels of the Carnival.
We a pine-grove did prefer

To a marble theatre,
Could with gods on mallows dine,
Nor cared for spices or for wine.
Wreaths of mist and rainbow spanned,
Arch on arch, the grimmest land;
Whistle of a woodland bird
Made the pulses dance,
Note of horn in valleys heard
Filled the region with romance.

None can tell how sweet,
How virtuous, the morning air;
Every accent vibrates well;
Not alone the wood-bird's call,
Or shouting boys that chase their ball,
Pass the height of minstrel skill,
But the ploughman's thoughtless cry,
Lowing oxen, sheep that bleat,
And the joiner's hammer-beat,
Softened are above their will.
All grating discords melt,
No dissonant note is dealt,
And though thy voice be shrill
Like rasping file on steel,
Such is the temper of the air,
Echo waits with art and care,
And will the faults of song repair.

So by remote Superior Lake,
And by resounding Mackinac,
When northern storms the forest shake,
And billows on the long beach break,
The artful Air doth separate
Note by note all sounds that grate,
Smothering in her ample breast
All but godlike words,
Reporting to the happy ear
Only purified accords.
Strangely wrought from barking waves,
Soft music daunts the Indian braves, –
Convent-chanting which the child
Hears pealing from the panther's cave
And the impenetrable wild.

One musician is sure,
His wisdom will not fail,
He has not tasted wine impure,
Nor bent to passion frail.
Age cannot cloud his memory,
Nor grief untune his voice,
Ranging down the ruled scale
From tone of joy to inward wail,
Tempering the pitch of all
In his windy cave.
He all the fables knows,

And in their causes tells, –
Knows Nature's rarest moods,
Ever on her secret broods.
The Muse of men is coy,
Oft courted will not come;
In palaces and market squares
Entreated, she is dumb;
But my minstrel knows and tells
The counsel of the gods,
Knows of Holy Book the spells,
Knows the law of Night and Day,
And the heart of girl and boy,
The tragic and the gay,
And what is writ on Table Round
Of Arthur and his peers,
What sea and land discoursing say
In sidereal years.
He renders all his lore
In numbers wild as dreams,
Modulating all extremes, –
What the spangled meadow saith
To the children who have faith;
Only to children children sing,
Only to youth will spring be spring.

Who is the Bard thus magnified?
When did he sing? and where abide?

Chief of song where poets feast
Is the wind-harp which thou seest
In the casement at my side.

Æolian harp,
How strangely wise thy strain!
Gay for youth, gay for youth,
(Sweet is art, but sweeter truth,)
In the hall at summer eve
Fate and Beauty skilled to weave.
From the eager opening strings
Rung loud and bold the song.
Who but loved the wind-harp's note?
How should not the poet doat
On its mystic tongue,
With its primeval memory,
Reporting what old minstrels said
Of Merlin locked the harp within, –
Merlin paying the pain of sin,
Pent in a dungeon made of air, –
And some attain his voice to hear,
Words of pain and cries of fear,
But pillowed all on melody,
As fits the griefs of bards to be.
And what if that all-echoing shell,
Which thus the buried Past can tell,
Should rive the Future, and reveal

What his dread folds would fain conceal?
It shares the secret of the earth,
And of the kinds that owe her birth.
Speaks not of self that mystic tone,
But of the Overgods alone:
It trembles to the cosmic breath, –
As it heareth, so it saith;
Obeying meek the primal Cause,
It is the tongue of mundane laws.
And this, at least, I dare affirm,
Since genius too has bound and term,
There is no bard in all the choir,
Not Homer's self, the poet sire,
Wise Milton's odes of pensive pleasure,
Or Shakspeare, whom no mind can measure,
Nor Collins' verse of tender pain,
Nor Byron's clarion of disdain,
Scott, the delight of generous boys,
Or Wordsworth, Pan's recording voice, –
Not one of all can put in verse,
Or to this presence could rehearse,
The sights and voices ravishing
The boy knew on the hills in spring,
When pacing through the oaks he heard
Sharp queries of the sentry-bird,
The heavy grouse's sudden whir,
The rattle of the kingfisher;

Saw bonfires of the harlot flies
In the lowland, when day dies;
Or marked, benighted and forlorn,
The first far signal-fire of morn.
These syllables that Nature spoke,
And the thoughts that in him woke,
Can adequately utter none
Save to his ear the wind-harp lone.
And best can teach its Delphian chord
How Nature to the soul is moored,
If once again that silent string,
As erst it wont, would thrill and ring.

Not long ago, at eventide,
It seemed, so listening, at my side
A window rose, and, to say sooth,
I looked forth on the fields of youth:
I saw fair boys bestriding steeds,
I knew their forms in fancy weeds,
Long, long concealed by sundering fates,
Mates of my youth, – yet not my mates,
Stronger and bolder far than I,
With grace, with genius, well attired,
And then as now from far admired,
Followed with love
They knew not of,
With passion cold and shy.

O joy, for what recoveries rare!
Renewed, I breathe Elysian air,
See youth's glad mates in earliest bloom, –
Break not my dream, obtrusive tomb!
Or teach thou, Spring! the grand recoil
Of life resurgent from the soil
Wherein was dropped the mortal spoil.

Soft on the south-wind sleeps the haze:
So on thy broad mystic van
Lie the opal-colored days,
And waft the miracle to man.
Soothsayer of the eldest gods,
Repairer of what harms betide,
Revealer of the inmost powers
Prometheus proffered, Jove denied;
Disclosing treasures more than true,
Or in what far to-morrow due;
Speaking by the tongues of flowers,
By the ten-tongued laurel speaking,
Singing by the oriole songs,
Heart of bird the man's heart seeking;
Whispering hints of treasure hid
Under Morn's unlifted lid,
Islands looming just beyond
The dim horizon's utmost bound; –
Who can, like thee, our rags upbraid,

Or taunt us with our hope decayed?
Or who like thee persuade,
Making the splendor of the air,
The morn and sparkling dew, a snare?
Or who resent
Thy genius, wiles, and blandishment?

There is no orator prevails
To beckon or persuade
Like thee the youth or maid:
Thy birds, thy songs, thy brooks, thy gales,
Thy blooms, thy kinds,
Thy echoes in the wilderness,
Soothe pain, and age, and love's distress,
Fire fainting will, and build heroic minds.

For thou, O Spring! canst renovate
All that high God did first create.
Be still his arm and architect,
Rebuild the ruin, mend defect;
Chemist to vamp old worlds with new,
Coat sea and sky with heavenlier blue,
New-tint the plumage of the birds,
And slough decay from grazing herds,
Sweep ruins from the scarped mountain,
Cleanse the torrent at the fountain,
Purge alpine air by towns defiled,

Bring to fair mother fairer child,
Not less renew the heart and brain,
Scatter the sloth, wash out the stain,
Make the aged eye sun-clear,
To parting soul bring grandeur near.
Under gentle types, my Spring
Masks the might of Nature's king,
An energy that searches thorough
From Chaos to the dawning morrow;
Into all our human plight,
The soul's pilgrimage and flight;
In city or in solitude,
Step by step, lifts bad to good,
Without halting, without rest,
Lifting Better up to Best;
Planting seeds of knowledge pure,
Through earth to ripen, through heaven endure.

THE ADIRONDACS
A Journal

Dedicated to My Fellow-Travellers in August, 1858

> Wise and polite, – and if I drew
> Their several portraits, you would own
> Chaucer had no such worthy crew,
> Nor Boccace in Decameron.

We crossed Champlain to Keeseville with our friends,
Thence, in strong country carts, rode up the forks
Of the Ausable stream, intent to reach
The Adirondac lakes. At Martin's Beach
We chose our boats; each man a boat and guide, –
Ten men, ten guides, our company all told.

Next morn, we swept with oars the Saranac,
With skies of benediction, to Round Lake,
Where all the sacred mountains drew around us,
Taháwus, Seaward, MacIntyre, Baldhead,
And other Titans without muse or name.
Pleased with these grand companions, we glide on,
Instead of flowers, crowned with a wreath of hills,
And made our distance wider, boat from boat,
As each would hear the oracle alone.
By the bright morn the gay flotilla slid
Through files of flags that gleamed like bayonets,

Through gold-moth-haunted beds of pickerel-flower,
Through scented banks of lilies white and gold,
Where the deer feeds at night, the teal by day,
On through the Upper Saranac, and up
Père Raquette stream, to a small tortuous pass
Winding through grassy shallows in and out,
Two creeping miles of rushes, pads, and sponge,
To Follansbee Water, and the Lake of Loons.

Northward the length of Follansbee we rowed,
Under low mountains, whose unbroken ridge
Pondrous with beechen forest sloped the shore.
A pause and council: then, where near the head
On the east a bay makes inward to the land
Between two rocky arms, we climb the bank,
And in the twilight of the forest noon
Wield the first axe these echoes ever heard.
We cut young trees to make our poles and thwarts,
Barked the white spruce to weatherfend the roof,
Then struck a light, and kindled the camp-fire.

The wood was sovran with centennial trees, –
Oak, cedar, maple, poplar, beech and fir,

Linden and spruce. In strict society
Three conifers, white, pitch, and Norway pine,
Five-leaved, three-leaved, and two-leaved, grew
    thereby.
Our patron pine was fifteen feet in girth,
The maple eight, beneath its shapely tower.

  'Welcome!' the wood god murmured through the
    leaves, –
'Welcome, though late, unknowing, yet known to me.'
Evening drew on; stars peeped through maple-boughs,
Which o'erhung, like a cloud, our camping fire.
Decayed millennial trunks, like moonlight flecks,
Lit with phosphoric crumbs the forest floor.

  Ten scholars, wonted to lie warm and soft
In well-hung chambers daintily bestowed,
Lie here on hemlock-boughs, like Sacs and Sioux,
And greet unanimous the joyful change.
So fast will Nature acclimate her sons,
Though late returning to her pristine ways.
Off soundings, seamen do not suffer cold;
And, in the forest, delicate clerks, unbrowned,
Sleep on the fragrant brush, as on down-beds.
Up with the dawn, they fancied the light air
That circled freshly in their forest dress
Made them to boys again. Happier that they

Slipped off their pack of duties, leagues behind,
At the first mounting of the giant stairs.
No placard on these rocks warned to the polls,
No door-bell heralded a visitor,
No courier waits, no letter came or went,
Nothing was ploughed, or reaped, or bought, or sold;
The frost might glitter, it would blight no crop,
The falling rain will spoil no holiday.
We were made freemen of the forest laws,
All dressed, like Nature, fit for her own ends,
Essaying nothing she cannot perform.

In Adirondac lakes,
At morn or noon, the guide rows bareheaded:
Shoes, flannel shirt, and kersey trousers make
His brief toilette: at night, or in the rain,
He dons a surcoat which he doffs at morn:
A paddle in the right hand, or an oar,
And in the left, a gun, his needful arms.
By turns we praised the stature of our guides,
Their rival strength and suppleness, their skill
To row, to swim, to shoot, to build a camp,
To climb a lofty stem, clean without boughs
Full fifty feet, and bring the eaglet down:
Temper to face wolf, bear, or catamount,
And wit to trap or take him in his lair.
Sound, ruddy men, frolic and innocent,

In winter, lumberers; in summer, guides;
Their sinewy arms pull at the oar untired
Three times ten thousand strokes, from morn to eve.

Look to yourselves, ye polished gentlemen!
No city airs or arts pass current here.
Your rank is all reversed: let men of cloth
Bow to the stalwart churls in overalls:
They are the doctors of the wilderness,
And we the low-prized laymen.
In sooth, red flannel is a saucy test
Which few can put on with impunity.
What make you, master, fumbling at the oar?
Will you catch crabs? Truth tries pretension here.
The sallow knows the basket-maker's thumb;
The oar, the guide's. Dare you accept the tasks
He shall impose, to find a spring, trap foxes,
Tell the sun's time, determine the true north,
Or stumbling on through vast self-similar woods
To thread by night the nearest way to camp?

Ask you, how went the hours?
All day we swept the lake, searched every cove,
North from Camp Maple, south to Osprey Bay,
Watching when the loud dogs should drive in deer,
Or whipping its rough surface for a trout;
Or bathers, diving from the rock at noon;

Challenging Echo by our guns and cries;
Or listening to the laughter of the loon;
Or, in the evening twilight's latest red,
Beholding the procession of the pines;
Or, later yet, beneath a lighted jack,
In the boat's bows, a silent night-hunter
Stealing with paddle to the feeding-grounds
Of the red deer, to aim at a square mist.
Hark to that muffled roar! a tree in the woods
Is fallen: but hush! it has not scared the buck
Who stands astonished at the meteor light,
Then turns to bound away, – is it too late?

Sometimes we tried our rifles at a mark,
Six rods, sixteen, twenty, or forty-five;
Sometimes our wits at sally and retort,
With laughter sudden as the crack of rifle;
Or parties scaled the near acclivities
Competing seekers of a rumored lake,
Whose unauthenticated waves we named
Lake Probability, – our carbuncle,
Long sought, not found.

                              Two Doctors in the camp
Dissected the slain deer, weighed the trout's brain,
Captured the lizard, salamander, shrew,
Crab, mice, snail, dragon-fly, minnow, and moth;

Insatiate skill in water or in air
Waved the scoop-net, and nothing came amiss;
The while, one leaden pot of alcohol
Gave an impartial tomb to all the kinds.
Not less the ambitious botanist sought plants,
Orchis and gentian, fern, and long whip-scirpus,
Rosy polygonum, lake-margin's pride,
Hypnum and hydnum, mushroom, sponge, and moss,
Or harebell nodding in the gorge of falls.
Above, the eagle flew, the osprey screamed,
The raven croaked, owls hooted, the woodpecker
Loud hammered, and the heron rose in the swamp.
As water poured through hollows of the hills
To feed this wealth of lakes and rivulets,
So Nature shed all beauty lavishly
From her redundant horn.

                              Lords of this realm,
Bounded by dawn and sunset, and the day
Rounded by hours where each outdid the last
In miracles of pomp, we must be proud,
As if associates of the sylvan gods.
We seemed the dwellers of the zodiac,
So pure the Alpine element we breathed,
So light, so lofty pictures came and went.
We trode on air, contemned the distant town,
Its timorous ways, big trifles, and we planned

That we should build, hard-by, a spacious lodge,
And how we should come hither with our sons,
Hereafter, – willing they, and more adroit.

   Hard fare, hard bed, and comic misery, –
The midge, the blue-fly, and the mosquito
Painted our necks, hands, ankles, with red bands:
But, on the second day, we heed them not,
Nay, we saluted them Auxiliaries,
Whom earlier we had chid with spiteful names.
For who defends our leafy tabernacle
From bold intrusion of the travelling crowd, –
Who but the midge, mosquito, and the fly,
Which past endurance sting the tender cit,
But which we learn to scatter with a smudge,
Or baffle by a veil, or slight by scorn?

   Our foaming ale we drunk from hunters' pans,
Ale, and a sup of wine. Our steward gave
Venison and trout, potatoes, beans, wheat-bread;
All ate like abbots, and, if any missed
Their wonted convenance, cheerly hid the loss
With hunters' appetite and peals of mirth.
And Stillman, our guides' guide, and Commodore,
Crusoe, Crusader, Pius Æneas, said aloud,
'Chronic dyspepsia never came from eating
Food indigestible': – then murmured some,
Others applauded him who spoke the truth.

Nor doubt but visitings of graver thought
Checked in these souls the turbulent heyday
'Mid all the hints and glories of the home.
For who can tell what sudden privacies
Were sought and found, amid the hue and cry
Of scholars furloughed from their tasks, and let
Into this Oreads' fended Paradise,
As chapels in the city's thoroughfares,
Whither gaunt Labor slips to wipe his brow,
And meditate a moment on Heaven's rest.
Judge with what sweet surprises Nature spoke
To each apart, lifting her lovely shows
To spiritual lessons pointed home.
And as through dreams in watches of the night,
So through all creatures in their form and ways
Some mystic hint accosts the vigilant
Not clearly voiced, but waking a new sense
Inviting to new knowledge, one with old.
Hark to that petulant chirp! what ails the warbler?
Mark his capricious ways to draw the eye.
Now soar again. What wilt thou, restless bird,
Seeking in that chaste blue a bluer light,
Thirsting in that pure for a purer sky?

And presently the sky is changed; O world!
What pictures and what harmonies are thine!
The clouds are rich and dark, the air serene,

So like the soul of me, what if 't were me?
A melancholy better than all mirth.
Comes the sweet sadness at the retrospect,
Or at the foresight of obscurer years?
Like yon slow-sailing cloudy promontory,
Whereon the purple iris dwells in beauty
Superior to all its gaudy skirts.
And, that no day of life may lack romance,
The spiritual stars rise nightly, shedding down
A private beam into each several heart.
Daily the bending skies solicit man,
The seasons chariot him from this exile,
The rainbow hours bedeck his glowing chair,
The storm-winds urge the heavy weeks along,
Suns haste to set, that so remoter lights
Beckon the wanderer to his vaster home.

With a vermilion pencil mark the day
When of our little fleet three cruising skiffs
Entering Big Tupper, bound for the foaming Falls
Of loud Bog River, suddenly confront
Two of our mates returning with swift oars.
One held a printed journal waving high
Caught from a late-arriving traveller,
Big with great news, and shouted the report
For which the world had waited, now firm fact,
Of the wire-cable laid beneath the sea,

And landed on our coast, and pulsating
With ductile fire. Loud, exulting cries
From boat to boat, and to the echoes round,
Greet the glad miracle. Thought's new-found path
Shall supplement henceforth all trodden ways,
Match God's equator with a zone of art,
And lift man's public action to a height
Worthy the enormous cloud of witnesses,
When linked hemispheres attest his deed.
We have few moments in the longest life
Of such delight and wonder as there grew, –
Nor yet unsuited to that solitude:
A burst of joy, as if we told the fact
To ears intelligent; as if gray rock
And cedar grove and cliff and lake should know
This feat of wit, this triumph of mankind;
As if we men were talking in a vein
Of sympathy so large, that ours was theirs,
And a prime end of the most subtle element
Were fairly reached at last. Wake, echoing caves!
Bend nearer, faint day-moon! Yon thundertops,
Let them hear well! 't is theirs as much as ours.

    A spasm throbbing through the pedestals
Of Alp and Andes, isle and continent,
Urging astonished Chaos with a thrill
To be a brain, or serve the brain of man.

The lightning has run masterless too long;
He must to school, and learn his verb and noun,
And teach his nimbleness to earn his wage,
Spelling with guided tongue man's messages
Shot through the weltering pit of the salt sea.
And yet I marked, even in the manly joy
Of our great-hearted Doctor in his boat,
(Perchance I erred,) a shade of discontent;
Or was it for mankind a generous shame,
As of a luck not quite legitimate,
Since fortune snatched from wit the lion's part?
Was it a college pique of town and gown,
As one within whose memory it burned
That not academicians, but some lout,
Found ten years since the Californian gold?
And now, again, a hungry company
Of traders, led by corporate sons of trade,
Perversely borrowing from the shop the tools
Of science, not from the philosophers,
Had won the brightest laurel of all time.
'T was always thus, and will be; hand and head
Are ever rivals: but, though this be swift,
The other slow, – this the Prometheus,
And that the Jove, – yet, howsoever hid,
It was from Jove the other stole his fire,
And, without Jove, the good had never been.
It is not Iroquois or cannibals,

But ever the free race with front sublime,
And these instructed by their wisest too,
Who do the feat, and lift humanity.
Let not him mourn who best entitled was,
Nay, mourn not one: let him exult,
Yea, plant the tree that bears best apples, plant,
And water it with wine, nor watch askance
Whether thy sons or strangers eat the fruit:
Enough that mankind eat, and are refreshed.

We flee away from cities, but we bring
The best of cities with us, these learned classifiers,
Men knowing what they seek, armed eyes of experts.
We praise the guide, we praise the forest life;
But will we sacrifice our dear-bought lore
Of books and arts and trained experiment,
Or count the Sioux a match for Agassiz?
O no, not we! Witness the shout that shook
Wild Tupper Lake; witness the mute all-hail
The joyful traveller gives, when on the verge
Of craggy Indian wilderness he hears
From a log-cabin stream Beethoven's notes
On the piano, played with master's hand.
'Well done!' he cries; 'the bear is kept at bay,
The lynx, the rattlesnake, the flood, the fire;
All the fierce enemies, ague, hunger, cold,
This thin spruce roof, this clayed log-wall,

This wild plantation will suffice to chase.
Now speed the gay celerities of art,
What in the desert was impossible
Within four walls is possible again, –
Culture and libraries, mysteries of skill,
Traditioned fame of masters, eager strife
Of keen competing youths, joined or alone
To outdo each other, and extort applause.
Mind wakes a new-born giant from her sleep.
Twirl the old wheels! Time takes fresh start again,
On for a thousand years of genius more.'

The holidays were fruitful, but must end;
One August evening had a cooler breath;
Into each mind intruding duties crept;
Under the cinders burned the fires of home;
Nay, letters found us in our paradise;
So in the gladness of the new event
We struck our camp, and left the happy hills.
The fortunate star that rose on us sank not;
The prodigal sunshine rested on the land,
The rivers gambolled onward to the sea,
And Nature, the inscrutable and mute,
Permitted on her infinite repose
Almost a smile to steal to cheer her sons,
As if one riddle of the Sphinx were guessed.

From *The Poet*

... the poet is representative. He stands among partial men for the complete man, and apprises us not of his wealth, but of the common-wealth. The young man reveres men of genius, because, to speak truly, they are more himself than he is. They receive of the soul as he also receives, but they more. Nature enhances her beauty, to the eye of loving men, from their belief that the poet is beholding her shows at the same time. He is isolated among his contemporaries, by truth and by his art, but with this consolation in his pursuits, that they will draw all men sooner or later. For all men live by truth, and stand in need of expression. In love, in art, in avarice, in politics, in labour, in games, we study to utter our painful secret. The man is only half himself, the other half is his expression.

Notwithstanding this necessity to be published, adequate expression is rare. I know not how it is that we need an interpreter; but the great majority of men seem to be minors, who have not yet come into possession of their own, or mutes, who cannot report the conversation they have had with nature. There is no man who does not anticipate a supersensual utility in the sun, and stars, earth, and water. These stand and wait to render him a peculiar service. But there is some obstruction, or some excess of phlegm in our constitution, which does not suffer them to yield the due effect. The impressions of nature fall on us too feebly to make us artists. Every touch should thrill. Every man should be so much an artist, that he could report in conversation what had befallen him. Yet, in our experience, the rays or appulses have sufficient force to arrive at the senses, but not enough to reach the quick, and compel the reproduction of themselves in speech. The poet is the person in whom these powers are in balance, the man without impediment, who sees and handles that which others dream of, traverses the whole scale of experience, and is representative of man, in virtue of being the largest power to receive and to impart.

For the Universe has three children, born at one time, which reappear, under different names, in every system of thought, whether they be called cause, operation, and effect; or, more poetically, Jove, Pluto, Neptune; or, theologically, the Father, the Spirit, and the Son; but which we will call here, the Knower, the Doer, and the Sayer. These stand respectively for the love of truth, the love of good, and the love of beauty. These three are equal. Each is that which he is essentially, so that he cannot be surmounted or analyzed, and each of these three has the power of the others latent in him, and his own patent.

The poet is the sayer, the namer, and represents beauty. He is a sovereign, and stands on the centre.

For the world is not painted, or adorned, but is from the beginning beautiful; and God has not made some beautiful things, but Beauty is the creator of the universe. Therefore the poet is not any permissive potentate, but is emperor in his own right. Criticism is infested with a cant of materialism, which assumes that manual skill and activity is the first merit of all men, and disparages such as say and do not, overlooking the fact, that some men namely, poets, are natural sayers, sent into the world to the end of expression, and it confounds them with those whose province is action, but who quit it to imitate the sayers. But Homer's words are as costly and admirable to Homer, as Agamemnon's victories are to Agamemnon. The poet does not wait for the hero or the sage, but, as they act and think primarily, so he writes primarily what will and must be spoken, reckoning the others, though primaries also, yet, in respect to him, secondaries and servants; as sitters or models in the studio of a painter, or as assistants who bring building materials to an architect.

For poetry was all written before time was, and whenever we are so finely organized that we can penetrate into that region where the air is music, we hear those primal warblings, and attempt to write them down, but we lose ever and anon a word, or a verse, and substitute something of our own, and thus miswrite the poem. The men of more delicate ear write down these cadences more faithfully, and these transcripts, though imperfect, become the songs of the nations. For nature is as truly beautiful as it is good, or as it is reasonable, and must as much appear, as it must be done, or be known. Words and deeds are quite indifferent modes of the divine energy. Words are also actions, and actions are a kind of words.

The sign and credentials of the poet are, that he announces that which no man foretold. He is the true and only doctor; he knows and tells; he is the only teller of news, for he was present and privy to the appearance which he describes. He is a beholder of ideas, and an utterer of the necessary and causal. We do not speak now of men of poetical talents, or of industry and skill in metre, but of the true poet. I took part in a conversation the other day, concerning a recent writer of lyrics, a man of subtle mind, whose head appeared to be a music-box of delicate tunes and rhythms, and whose skill, and command of language, we could not sufficiently praise. But when the question arose, whether he were not only a lyrist, but a poet, we were obliged to confess that he is plainly a contemporary, not an eternal man. He does not stand out of our low limitations, like a Chimborazo under the line, running up from the torrid base through all the climates of the globe, with belts of the herbage of every latitude on its high and mottled sides; but this genuis is the landscape garden of a modern house, adorned with fountains and statues, with well-bred men and women standing and sitting in the walks and terraces. We hear, through all the varied music, the ground-tone of conventional life. Our poets are men of talents who sing, and not the children of music. The argument is secondary, the finish of the verses is primary.

For it is not metres, but a metre-making argument, that makes a poem, – a thought so passionate and alive, that, like the spirit of a plant or an animal, it has an architecture of its own, and adorns nature with a new thing. The thought and the form are equal in the order of time, but in the order of genesis the thought is prior to the form. The poet has a new thought: he has a whole new experience to unfold; he will tell us how it was with him, and all men will be the richer in his fortune ...

... Every man is so far a poet as to be susceptible of these enchantments of nature: for all men have the thoughts of which the universe is the celebration. I find that the fascination resides in the symbol. Who loves nature? Who does not? Is it only poets, and men of leisure and cultivation, who live with her? No; but also hunters, farmers, grooms, and butchers, though they express their affection in their choice of life, and not in their choice of words. The writer wonders what the coachman or the hunter values in riding, in horses, and dogs. It is not superficial qualities. When you talk with him, he holds these at as slight a rate as you. His worship is sympathetic: he has no definitions, but he is commanded in nature, by the living power which he feels to be there present. No imitation, or playing of these things, would content him; he loves the earnest of the north-wind, of rain, of stone, and wood, and iron. A beauty not explicable is dearer than a beauty which we can see to the end of. It is nature the symbol, nature certifying the supernatural, body overflowed by life, which he worships with coarse, but sincere rites.

The inwardness, and mystery, of this attachment, drives men of every class to the use of emblems. The schools of poets, and philosophers, are not more intoxicated with their symbols, than the populace with theirs. In our political parties, compute the power of badges and emblems. See the great ball which they roll from Baltimore to Bunker hill! In the political processions, Lowell goes in a loom, and Lynn in a shoe, and Salem in a ship. Witness the cider-barrel, the log-cabin, the hickory-stick, the palmetto, and all the cognizances of party. See the power of national emblems. Some stars, lilies, leopards, a crescent, a lion, an eagle, or other figure, which came into credit God knows how, on an old rag of bunting, blowing in the wind, on a fort, at the ends of the earth, shall make the blood tingle under the rudest, or the most conventional exterior. The people fancy they hate poetry, and they are all poets and mystics!

Beyond this universality of the symbolic language, we are apprised of the divineness of this superior use of things, (whereby the world is a temple, whose walls are covered with emblems, pictures, and commandments of the Deity,) in this, that there is no fact in nature which does not carry the whole sense of nature; and the distinctions which we make in events, and in affairs, of low and high, honest and base, disappear when nature is used as a symbol. Thought makes every thing fit for use. The vocabulary of an omniscient man would embrace words and images excluded from polite conversation. What would be base, or even obscene, to the obscene, becomes illustrious, spoken in a new connection of thought. The piety of the Hebrew prophets purges their grossness. The circumcision is an example of the power of poetry to raise the low and offensive. Small and mean things serve as well as great symbols. The meaner the type by which a law is expressed, the more pungent it is, and the more lasting in the memories of men: just as we choose the smallest box, or case, in which any needful utensil can be carried. Bare lists of words are found suggestive to an imaginative and excited mind; as it is related of Lord Chatham, that he was accustomed to read in Baily's Dictionary when he was preparing to speak in Parliament. The poorest experience is rich enough for all the purposes of expressing thought. Why covet a knowledge of new facts? Day and night, house and garden, a few books, a few actions, serve us as well as would all trades and all spectacles. We are far from having exhausted the significance of the few symbols we use. We can come to use them yet with a terrible simplicity. It does not need that a poem should be long. Every word was once a poem. Every new relation is a new word. Also, we use defects and deformities to a sacred purpose, – so expressing our sense that the evils of the world are such only to the evil eye. In the old mythology, mythologists observe, defects are ascribed to divine natures, as lameness to Vulcan, blindness to Cupid, and the like, to signify exuberances.

It is dislocation and detachment from the life of God that makes things ugly, and the poet, who re-attaches things to nature and the Whole, – re-attaching even artificial things, and violations of nature, to nature, by a deeper insight, – disposes very easily of the most disagreeable facts. Readers of poetry see the factory-village, and the railway, and fancy that the poetry of the landscape is broken up by these, – for these works of art are not yet consecrated in their reading; but the poet sees them fall within the great order not less than the hive, or the spider's geometrical web. Nature adopts them very fast into her vital circles, and the gliding train of cars she loves like her own. Besides, in a centred

mind, it signifies nothing how many mechanical inven-
tions you exhibit. Though you add millions, and never
so surprising, the fact of mechanics has not gained a
grain's weight. The spiritual fact remains unalterable,
by many or by few particulars; as no mountain is of any
appreciable height to break the curve of the sphere ...

The world being thus put under the mind for verb
and noun, the poet is he who can articulate it. For,
though life is great, and fascinates, and absorbs, – and
though all men are intelligent of the symbols through
which it is named, – yet they cannot originally use them.
We are symbols, and inhabit symbols; workmen, work,
and tools, words and things, birth and death, all are
emblems; but we sympathize with the symbols, and,
being infatuated with the economical uses of things, we
do not know that they are thoughts. The poet, by an
ulterior intellectual perception, gives them a power
which makes their old use forgotten, and puts eyes, and
a tongue, into every dumb and inanimate object. He
perceives the independence of the thought on the
symbol, – the stability of the thought, the accidency
and fugitiveness of the symbol. As the eyes of Lyncæus
were said to see through the earth, so the poet turns
the world to glass, and shows us all things in their
right series and procession. For, through that better
perception, he stands one step nearer to things, and sees
the flowing or metamorphosis; perceives that thought is

multiform; that within the form of every creature is a force impelling it to ascend into a higher form: and, following with his eyes the life, uses the forms which express that life, and so his speech flows with the flowing of nature. All the facts of the animal economy, sex, nutriment, gestation, birth, growth, are symbols of the passage of the world into the soul of man, to suffer there a change, and reappear a new and higher fact. He uses forms according to the life, and not according to the form. This is true science. The poet alone knows astronomy, chemistry, vegetation, and animation; for he does not stop at these facts, but employs them as signs. He knows why the field of space was strown with these flowers we call suns and moons and stars; why the great deep is adorned with animals, with men, and gods; for, in every word he speaks he rides on them as the horses of thought.

By virtue of this science the poet is the Namer or Language-maker, naming things sometimes after their appearance, sometimes after their essence, and giving to every one its own name and not another's, thereby rejoicing the intellect, which delights in detachment or boundary. The poets made all the words, and therefore language is the archives of history, and, if we must say it, a sort of tomb of the muses. For, though the origin of most of our words is forgotten, each word was at first a stroke of genius, and obtained currency, because for the moment it symbolized the world to the first speaker and to the hearer. The etymologist finds the deadest word to have been once a brilliant picture. Language is fossil poetry. As the limestone of the continent consists of infinite masses of the shells of animalcules, so language is made up of images, or tropes, which now, in their secondary use, have long ceased to remind us of their poetic origin. But the poet names the thing because he sees it, or comes one step nearer to it than any other. This expression, or naming, is not art, but a second nature, grown out of the first, as a leaf out of a tree. What we call nature, is a certain self-regulated motion or change; and nature does all things by her own hands, and does not leave another to baptize her, but baptizes herself; and this through the metamorphosis again ...

It is a secret which every intellectual man quickly learns, that, beyond the energy of his possessed and conscious intellect, he is capable of a new energy (as of an intellect doubled on itself), by abandonment to the nature of things; that, beside his privacy of power as an individual man, there is a great public power, on which he can draw, by unlocking, at all risks, his human doors, and suffering the ethereal tides to roll and circulate through him: then he is caught up into the life of the Universe, his speech is thunder, his thought is law, and his words are universally intelligible as the plants and animals. The poet knows that he speaks adequately, then only when he speaks somewhat wildly, or, 'with the flower of the mind;' not with the intellect, used as an organ, but with the intellect released from all service, and suffered to take its direction from its celestial life; or, as the ancients were wont to express themselves, not with intellect alone, but with the intellect inebriated by nectar. As the traveller who has lost his way, throws his reins on his horse's neck, and trusts to the instinct of the animal to find his road, so must we do with the divine animal who carries us through the world. For if in any manner we can stimulate this instinct, new passages are opened for us into nature, the mind flows into and through things hardest and highest, and the metamorphosis is possible...

If the imagination intoxicates the poet, it is not inactive in other men. The metamorphosis excites in the beholder an emotion of joy. The use of symbols has a certain power of emancipation and exhilaration for all men. We seem to be touched by a wand, which makes us dance and run about happily, like children. We are like persons who come out of a cave or cellar into the open air. This is the effect on us of tropes, fables, oracles, and all poetic forms ...

The poets are thus liberating gods. The ancient British bards had for the title of their order, 'Those who are free throughout the world.' They are free, and they make free. An imaginative book renders us much more service at first, by stimulating us through its tropes, than afterward, when we arrive at the precise sense of the author. I think nothing is of any value in books, excepting the transcendental and extraordinary. If a man is inflamed and carried away by his thought, to that degree that he forgets the authors and the public, and heeds only this one dream, which holds him like an insanity, let me read his paper, and you may have all the arguments, and histories, and criticism. All the value which attaches to Pythagoras, Paracelsus, Cornelius Agrippa, Cardan, Kepler, Swedenborg, Schelling, Oken, or any other who introduces questionable facts into his cosmogony, as angels, devils, magic, astrology, palmistry, mesmerism, and so on, is the certificate we have of departure from routine, and that here is a new witness. That also is the best success in conversation, the magic of liberty, which puts the world, like a ball, in our hands. How cheap even the liberty then seems; how mean to study, when an emotion communicates to the intellect the power to sap and upheave nature: how great the perspective! nations, times, systems, enter and disappear, like threads in tapestry of large figure and many colors; dream delivers us to dream, and, while the drunkenness lasts, we will sell our bed, our philosophy, our religion, in our opulence...